CASA SAN YSIDRO

CASA SAN YSIDRO

The Gutiérrez/Minge House
in Corrales, New Mexico

WARD ALAN MINGE

ALBUQUERQUE MUSEUM COLLECTION SERIES

MUSEUM OF NEW MEXICO PRESS
SANTA FE

The Museum of New Mexico Press is a division of the New Mexico Department of Cultural Affairs.

Director: Anna Gallegos
Editorial director: Lisa Pacheco
Art and production director: David Skolkin
Designed by Michael Motley
Composition: Set in Dante and Trajan
Manufactured in China
10 9 8 7 6 5 4 3 2 1

LCCN: 2017005228
ISBN 978-0-89013-625-6 hardcover

MUSEUM OF NEW MEXICO PRESS
PO Box 2087
Santa Fe, New Mexico 87504
mnmpress.org

Frontispiece (p. 2): Higinio V. Gonzales, Hispanic New Mexican nicho collected in Chávez, mid-nineteenth to early twentieth century. 32 11/16 × 31 7/8 × 13 5/8 in. José Benito Ortega, Hispanic New Mexican bulto of San José, ca. 1880. 15 3/16 × 4 11/16 × 13 5/8 in. Photograph by David Nufer. Gift of Ward Alan and Shirley Jolly Minge (1997.51.10).

CONTENTS

FOREWORD

Cathy L. Wright

WHEN I ACCEPTED THE POSITION AS DIRECTOR of the Albuquerque Museum in 2006, I was delighted that within its management was the Gutiérrez / Minge historic house, Casa San Ysidro. I had first visited Ward Alan and Shirley Minge at Casa in the early 1980s with a group of docents from the Taylor Museum in Colorado Springs. I never forgot the experience of being transported back to an earlier time in New Mexico, through its architectural features and wonderful furnishings so carefully gathered together in this living museum. It reaffirmed for me a longtime interest in the arts and cultures of the Southwest, and I know it still touches visitors in the same way to this day. It is a New Mexico treasure. Walking through the *zaguán* gates, visitors are instantly transported to a place where fire is needed for warmth, light, and cooking; food is raised in a kitchen garden or corral; and family and friends come together for worship, house-raising, plowing, and parties. At Casa one can relax a little, smile more deeply, and envision more clearly what life was like in eighteenth- and nineteenth-century Corrales.

What makes Casa special is its picturesque bosque location at 973 Old Church Road within the agricultural village of Corrales, New Mexico. This close-knit and vocal community cares about its architecture, acequias, arts, environment, plants and animals, and the role the village has played in the history of the central Rio Grande valley. Corraleños—especially the Gonzales and Gutiérrez families—cared for the land, donated property for the Old Church, built and raised families in Casa San Ysidro, planted trees and vines that still produce fruit, grew and harvested crops, sheared sheep and wove blankets, served in our nation's wars, and are buried in the nearby camposanto. Casa is significant to the people of Corrales because it represents cultural heritage and identity for many of its residents, and a lifestyle ideal for many others.

< FIGURE A
Dining room, 2012. Photograph by David Nufer.

FIGURE B
Meeting a burro, 2012. Photograph by David Nufer.

Casa San Ysidro is also special to families who live in the greater Albuquerque area. At the time Casa opened to the public in 1998, the rancho was unique in central New Mexico: the only museum interpreting Hispano life in a historic "placita-style" house, and the only historic house with Magic Bus tours—generously sponsored by Albuquerque Museum Foundation members—bringing thousands of schoolchildren through its huge zaguán doors for free.

For nearly two decades, the Albuquerque Museum has preserved and interpreted Casa San Ysidro and the Minges' stellar New Mexican collection. Acquired mostly through bond funds approved by the people of Albuquerque, the Minges' art, artifacts, and furnishings are incredible learning tools. The property and collections would not exist, however, without decades of effort by Alan and Shirley Minge to renovate the Gutiérrez property, expand its historic footprint in thoughtful ways, and work with Tony Garcia and others to collect objects that in many cases would have quite literally disintegrated within our generation. For more than forty years of mud, grit, grime, and perseverance, and for traveling miles of bumpy roads to purchase everything from cabins to *cazos*, we thank Alan and Shirley for their monumental efforts.

This book, compiled in honor of Casa San Ysidro's twentieth year as a public historic house museum, also honors Dr. Ward Alan Minge for his accomplishments as one of New Mexico's preeminent scholars of Spanish Colonial, Mexican, Territorial, and Pueblo history. Born on March 20, 1924, on a farm north of Waterville, Kansas, Alan served as a historian at Kirtland Air Force Base and was the first historian hired to help the Pueblos negotiate the maze of legal issues affecting tribal land and water rights. His independent research in our nation's archives established his expertise on Colonial and Mexican tinwork, ironwork, carpentry, weavings, Pueblo pottery, Navajo

FIGURE C
Jason Delgado Younis demonstrating tinwork, 2012. Photograph by David Nufer.

and Apache textiles and basketry, and other furnishings found in historic New Mexican homes. For more than sixty years of research, contributions to major publications, and patient documentation of the Minge Collection that continues today, we are eternally grateful to Alan.

Ward Alan Minge is the primary author of this book, which showcases Casa San Ysidro and the Ward Alan and Shirley Jolly Minge Collection. Alan is the only person who knows the property and its historical background inside out. Only Alan can tell the story of how its placita-style addition came together, and relate the sequencing of its renovation and construction between 1954 and 1996. Alan has not only written an authoritative and compelling story of his years creating Casa San Ysidro: The Gutiérrez/Minge House, but he has also contributed funds to help underwrite this publication and to fund future Casa endeavors. The book features photographs of Casa's rooms and furnishings compiled by the Albuquerque Museum's curator of history, Deborah C. Slaney, along with an introduction to the Minge Collection. Through this book we celebrate Ward Alan Minge's scholarly and architectural accomplishments in New Mexico.

This year, as we prepare to celebrate Casa's twenty-year anniversary and more than 140 years as the Gutiérrez House, the Albuquerque Museum has engaged in strategic planning with community members both local and regional. Our mission is to create strong long-term collaborations; to develop new community initiatives, public events, and programs featuring history and the arts; and ultimately to craft a sustainable financial future for Casa San Ysidro.

How rewarding it is to be part of a museum and historic site that fosters long-term relationships with scholars, art historians, and citizens of Corrales, and to support the preservation of New Mexico's cultural history. We encourage you to enjoy this book and experience for yourselves the gem that is Casa San Ysidro.

INTRODUCTION

CASA SAN YSIDRO AND THE WARD ALAN AND SHIRLEY JOLLY MINGE COLLECTION

Deborah C. Slaney

CASA SAN YSIDRO: THE GUTIÉRREZ / MINGE HOUSE is a charming historic house museum in Corrales, New Mexico. A satellite of the Albuquerque Museum operated jointly by the City of Albuquerque and the Village of Corrales, New Mexico, with support from Sandoval County and the State of New Mexico Historic Preservation Division, and affectionately known as "Casa," the property is home to one of the most comprehensive collections of New Mexican art and furnishings.

Like many historic properties in New Mexico, Casa San Ysidro's history and construction are delightfully complicated. Casa consists of four main components: (1) a Territorial period Greek Revival rancho built around 1875 by Jesús María Gutiérrez and renovated by Dr. Ward Alan Minge and his wife Shirley Jolly Minge, (2) additional adobe rooms designed and hand built by the Minges around a traditional eighteenth- to early-nineteenth-century-style *plazuela* using structural parts from significant at-risk historical buildings; (3) a re-created mid- to late-nineteenth-century corral surrounding a historic barn and cabins moved to the property by the Minges; and (4) a heritage field to the north of the rancho, protected from development by a conservation easement.

According to architectural historian Chris Wilson, citing a survey completed by archaeologist Mike Marshall in 1984 as well as recent salvage archaeology conducted on the property, there is also an archaeological component to Casa. Through the years, Alan had found artifacts that suggested a six hundred-year-long occupation history. Marshall's site survey report concluded, "The sample indicates the presence of a prehistoric Glaze A-D component of probably fourteenth–fifteenth century affinity and a post-Revolt reoccupation of probably early nineteenth century establishment with

< FIGURE 1
Jesús María Gutiérrez (seated) with daughter Dorella and others, ca. 1890. Courtesy Ramona Gutiérrez Holdeman via the Corrales Historical Society.

> FIGURE 2
Portrait of Encarnación Lucero Gutiérrez, mother of Jesús María Gutiérrez, 1895. Albright Art Parlors. Photograph by David Nufer. Gift of Ramona Gutiérrez Holdeman (2015.59.1).

a continuous occupation until today." Although these initial collections—described as corrugated and glazeware pottery; olive jar fragments; and ceramic, glass, and iron artifacts—no longer exist, recently discovered artifact scatters that include what appear to be Pohoge or Ogapoge Polychrome and Kapo Black or Hispanic Blackware potsherds, circa 1800, indicate the presence of an early nineteenth-century Pueblo or Hispano occupation of the site. Casa is identified as a property with archaeological and historical significance and is assigned site number LA50277 by the Museum of Indian Arts and Culture / Laboratory of Anthropology in Santa Fe.

Through conversations with Alan Minge and living Gutiérrez descendants, we know that by the 1870s the Gutiérrez family owned a large strip of land from the Rio Grande to the ceja (ridge) where runoff from the Rio Puerco originates. The Gutiérrez family could have owned the property as far back as 1778, when baptismal records for Sandia Pueblo Parish list a Juan Francisco Gutiérrez and his wife. Juan Francisco was likely descended from Felipe Gutiérrez, who was born around 1655–60, before the 1680 Pueblo Revolt, in the Rio Abajo, returning to the area in 1693, presumably with Don Diego de Vargas. The strip included land south of the cemetery. Family members owned at least two homes in the area: what is now Casa San Ysidro at 973 Old Church Road, and the Feliz and Bruna Gutiérrez Sandoval house at 984 Old Church Road.

While the construction year for Jesús María Gutiérrez's home is unknown, the Greek Revival adobe and *terrón* home dates to the 1870s or early 1880s, when this architectural style came into vogue in the central Rio Grande valley. Research conducted by Chris Wilson indicated that the property, on high ground, survived the flood of 1864. Some scholars believe that what the Minges purchased in 1954 was the rebuilt northeastern corner of an earlier structure that succumbed to earlier flooding and lack of repair (see fig. 15).

Gutiérrez descendant Ramona Gutiérrez Holdeman confirmed in 2015 that the original builder of Casa San Ysidro was Jesús María Gutiérrez of Corrales (fig. 1). Jesús María Gutiérrez was part of a nine-member family that included his father, Juan Francisco Gutiérrez; mother, Encarnación Lucero Gutiérrez; brothers Feliz, Tomás,

José León, and Pablo; and sisters Catalina and Dulcinea. His family contributed to the donation of land for the 1868 church and camposanto after a disastrous flood destroyed the original church, closer to the river. Jesús María's brother Feliz (1897–1964) served as a private in the army during World War I and is buried in the camposanto. Jesús María Gutiérrez eventually married Julianita Griego and had three children: daughters Bruna and Dorella, and son Napoleón. Napoleón worked as the village justice of the peace, and his daughter Bruna was a caretaker for the 1868 church.

By 1875, Jesús María's father, Juan Francisco Gutiérrez, was living on the site, either in Casa or in a previously existing dwelling, according to his great-granddaughter Stella Gutiérrez-Sandoval Mares. It is unknown if Juan Francisco's son, builder Jesús María Gutiérrez, ever lived at Casa. According to Florinda Gutiérrez, Feliz did live there, but according to Stella's daughter, Ramona Gutiérrez Holdeman, Jesús María's mother, Encarnación (fig. 2), never lived there (even if her husband Juan Francisco may have).

Dr. Minge recalls from conversations with Rosaura Gutiérrez that Jesús María's son Napoleón Gutiérrez and his wife Rosaura lived at Casa from the late 1800s to about 1905. Some family members have indicated that José Ignacio Gutiérrez (and presumably his wife, Stella) also lived there, but this is refuted by Ramona Gutiérrez Holdeman, who recalls instead that her great-aunt Catalina Córdova and her husband Higinio raised Rosaura, and that they gave Rosaura the house when they passed away (fig. 3). So Napoleón and Rosaura definitely lived there, and Rosaura also returned to live in and care for the house while the Minges owned it.

Sometime after 1905 Constancio Candelaria purchased the house from Napoleón and Rosaura, either directly or through Higinio Córdova, according to Constancio's son Felipe Candelaria. By the 1950s the house was owned by Napoleón's daughter Bruna, followed by Bruna's daughter, Inés Gutiérrez-Gurulé, who sold the property to the Minges in 1954 (fig. 4). Through these collected memories we learn that at least five generations of Gutiérrezes lived in the home prior to the Minges: Feliz and Napoleón, Catalina and Higinio Córdova, Rosaura, Bruna, and Inés Gutiérrez-Gurulé.

FIGURE 3
Gutiérrez family and friends, including José Ignacio and Stella Montoya Gutiérrez (seventh and third from right) and children, Gutiérrez General Merchandise, Corrales, ca. 1890. Gift of Patricia Gutiérrez (PA2008.10.1).

Occasional visitors to Casa also remember living there, including Lalla Candelaria Rinaldi, who was born in 1932. In 2015 she related that she lived at Casa as a child and moved away at the age of five. Rinaldi recalled that the upper kitchen was a third bedroom, and that there were two additional rooms to the south of the home, now gone. In the kitchen, she recalled, "I stood at this window, opened a hinge, and fed a horse through the window."

Alan Minge remembers, "The Gutiérrez family comes back occasionally and they want to see the bedroom where they slept as kids. Then the Griegos . . . when they visit, they love to come to [the *galería*] because they said as kids they used to dance in this hall. They'd come over here on Saturday nights and dance with the Gutiérrezes. What Hispanos are moved by is to find all this together in a meaningful way. This was their life."

Casa San Ysidro is unique for other reasons. It may be the only historic property in the state where the collections, as well as the structures, are listed on the State

FIGURE 4
Martin Minge, Charles Mullen, and Ward Alan Minge, 1967. Courtesy Ward Alan Minge.

Register of Cultural Properties. Ward Alan Minge and his wife, Shirley, spent nearly half a century renovating and preserving the Gutiérrez House. They also assembled a collection while Alan was earning a degree in Latin American history and working as a contract historian for Acoma, Sandia, Santa Ana, Santo Domingo, Zia, and Zuni Pueblos, and later as chief historian for Kirtland Air Force Base's weapons laboratory while Shirley served as a colonel in the army.

The Minges have been credited with having the foresight to collect and preserve utilitarian items that otherwise would have been destroyed or lost to time, dust, and rust. In the process of assembling the plazuela and corral, the Minges salvaged architectural elements from other historic structures in New Mexico—also cataloged into the collection—that were threatened by remodeling, demolition, or even fire. Their endeavor (often described by architects as a romantic re-creation) is part of the time-honored tradition of adaptive reuse that has existed for centuries in the central Rio Grande valley.

The Minges sold and donated objects from their collection to the Albuquerque Museum as early as the 1980s, and in the mid-1990s they decided to find a museum willing and able to oversee the property and collection long term. Their goal was to keep the collection intact and preserved within the state of New Mexico—a difficult task given the interest of major museums such as the Boston Museum of Fine Arts, the Peabody Museum of Archaeology and Ethnology at Harvard, and the National Museum of American History.

Through a successful General Obligation Bond fund approved by Albuquerque voters in 1995, the Albuquerque Museum purchased a majority of the Minge Collection in 1996. In 1997, the museum purchased much of the remaining collection, and the Minges completed a donation of the property to the museum that same year. Continuing Alan and Shirley's passionate work to teach others about New Mexico history by conducting tours of the exhibits and hosting special events, Casa San Ysidro officially opened to the public as a historic house museum in 1998. After Shirley's death in 2005, artifacts that remained as loans and others from Shirley's estate were also donated to or purchased by the museum, bringing the total to more than 1,800 objects in the Ward

Alan and Shirley Jolly Minge Collection. Today, Casa is one of only four public museums in the state with collections exhibited against a distinctly New Mexican architectural backdrop, enhancing its interpretive value beyond measure.

In 1978, historian Marc Simmons advised the New Mexico Cultural Properties Review Committee that the Ward Alan and Shirley Jolly Minge Collection was the best of its kind in the Southwest. The Minge Collection includes architectural elements, furniture, religious art, household tools and hardware, jewelry, Hispanic and Pueblo weavings and pottery, a transportation collection, and historic photographs.

The furniture collection includes major examples of Spanish Colonial, Folk Gothic, and New Mexico Empire carpentry produced during the seventeenth to nineteenth centuries. Metalwork from the Minge Collection is one of the most comprehensive, systematic collections of its kind in the Southwest and includes implements made of iron, gold, silver, and copper. The comprehensive weaving collection includes Navajo and Rio Grande textiles from northern Arizona to the middle Rio Grande to the San Luis Valley of Colorado. The Rio Grande *jerga* collection alone surpasses any other, worldwide. The santo collection includes retablos, bultos, and tin-framed depictions of San Ysidro Labrador, patron saint of agriculture and of Corrales, and other beloved saints by major eighteenth- and nineteenth-century *santeros*. Pottery includes rare utilitarian Hispano vessels as well as utilitarian and tourist pottery made by Acoma, Cochiti, Picuris, Santa Ana, Santa Clara, San Ildefonso, Zia, and Zuni potters. Basketry includes early Apache, Navajo, and Pueblo vessels for sifting, harvesting, water carrying, and storage. A small collection of wagons interprets Corrales's pre-railroad transportation history, while a small photograph collection documents Casa's construction history.

The Minge Collection was built in part through thoughtful purchases from dealer Tony Garcia, who acquired entire collections from Will Prince, Luz Chávez, Baca and Martínez family descendants, Isleta's Abeita family, and others, on behalf of the Minges. But Alan and Shirley have been equally proud of the many gifts of pottery and stonework from their friends at Acoma Pueblo, as well as presents from family, friends, and neighbors who appreciated their passion for New Mexico material culture. Today, the Museum actively works to enhance the collection through acquisitions that help interpret the Minge Collection, flesh out the Gutiérrez family history, and document Casa's archaeological record.

Casa San Ysidro is a lifetime member of the Corrales Historical Society and a partner in the National Endowment for the Arts Blue Star Museums program, which provides free admission for military veterans. Casa also partners with the National Trust for Historic Preservation to provide admission discounts for NTHP members. In 2010, Casa San Ysidro was designated by the National Park Service as a stopping point on El Camino Real de la Tierra Adentro National Interpretive Trail.

The Albuquerque Museum is grateful to the many entities and individuals who have contributed time and resources to Casa and this book, which honors Dr. Ward Alan Minge and his thoughtful and passionate contributions to the history and culture of New Mexico. Alan's willingness to share his story will help keep the history of the Gutiérrez/Minge House alive. We are also indebted to the City of Albuquerque, Albuquerque Museum Board of Trustees, Albuquerque Museum Foundation, Casa Advisory Committee, Casa San Ysidro docents and staff, Albuquerque Museum staff, Damian Andrus, Ed Boles, Corrales Historical Society, Mary Davis, Dawn Hall, Ward Alan Minge and the late Shirley Jolly Minge, James Moore, New Mexico Historic Preservation Division, David Nufer, Gene Peach, Robert Reck, Sandoval County Tourism, Matthew Schmader, and Nora Vanesky. We at the Museum are also grateful to Anna Gallegos, director, Lisa Pacheco, editorial director, and David Skolkin, art and production director, at the Museum of New Mexico Press and Michael Motley, book designer. Other sources of objects and photographs are noted in the image credits. Provenance for the collection is within what is now New Mexico, unless otherwise noted.

CHAPTER 1

WE FIND CASA

VISITORS TO CASA SAN YSIDRO HAVE OFTEN RAISED QUESTIONS. How did Casa come into being and why? What spawned my interest in Spanish history and culture? How were my wife Shirley and I able to accomplish such a project while pursuing our individual careers? What existed on the property worthy of preserving? What was done to render the building habitable? Visitors also expressed interest in the unfamiliar items in the collections. On considering the above and more, the simplest answer is that a number of circumstances brought about our commitment to restore Casa, including incidents of serendipity but also our love for preservation and feeling comfortable with our past. From childhood, Shirley and I were fascinated with old things and their histories. We met as undergraduates at the University of Denver in 1944. After World War II we moved to Central City, Colorado. One of the oldest towns in Colorado, and one whose miners had created remarkable buildings and houses, some quite opulent, Central City had become an artists' mecca. We were lucky to rent one of the oldest houses on Casey Street. For four years we furnished this Carpenter Gothic home while enjoying Metropolitan Opera performances imported in July and Broadway shows in August.

Trips in my army jeep over rugged mountain roads introduced us to other mining towns, some all but abandoned, with their fanciful storefronts, Victorian houses, hotels, vacant opera houses, and cemeteries, where we read epitaphs about plagues, mining tragedies, murders, and so much more. Leadville, at over ten thousand feet in elevation, was a big attraction; we hoped it would never change. The town is home to the historic Healy House, the Paris Hotel, and numerous Victorian homes.

< FIGURE 5
Casa San Ysidro, ca. 1959. Photograph by Walter Haussamen. Gift of Walter Haussamen (PA2002.10.5).

At the same time irresistible "finds"—especially at Denver's Goodwill store—helped to furnish the rental on Casey Street. The mountain towns were full of surprises as well. On a lark we drove all night to Leadville, where the following morning we found a notions store open. The owner had stacks of wallpaper all around the place, and she explained that a few days earlier she had discovered in an abandoned warehouse great stacks of nineteenth-century papers. The selections she showed us were unbelievably colorful and like new. Evidently there were complete sets of rolls, borders, and insets designed for specific rooms. She had assembled one, for example, that included lavish borders, apple-green panels streaming with violets and roses, and rolls meant for the ceiling festooned in pink roses. Toward each corner, a circle of such roses framed cherubs peering into the room—each a different portrait. We were able to buy borders for the rooms on Casey Street but could not afford the entire collection, alas.

In 1947 I attended summer school at the University of Mexico in Mexico City, and Shirley joined the army. I had been working in Latin American studies (history) at the University of Denver so I could arrange to stay in Mexico. That summer I began a deep, serious commitment to Hispanic culture and history. Shirley continued serving in the army while I returned to Denver and completed my undergraduate degree. I continued to occupy the Carpenter Gothic on Casey Street on weekends and summers and even earned some money as head bartender at Central City's Glory Hole Tavern.

I returned to Mexico City for graduate work in 1950, majoring in history at the University of the Americas. I lived nearby on the Paseo de la Reforma. In those days, professors from the University of Mexico also held classes at the University of the Americas while a new campus was being constructed for the University of Mexico. Colleges that had been located in colonial buildings downtown now moved out to the new campus beyond the city itself. From time to time, professors asked for the use of my jeep to visit remote villages and archaeological sites reachable often only on foot or on horseback. With their guidance and on my own, I experienced what I imagined was a bit of true Mexico. Here were village arts, markets and fiestas, and country churches. I learned that Mexico's folk arts were renowned treasures, that Picasso had one of the greatest collections of Mexican folk art, that the United Nations established a UNESCO branch in Pátzcuaro because of Mexico's traditions in the arts, and that these folk traditions are particularly strong in that area of the state of Michoacán.

FIGURE 6
Mexican cazo, 1689.
16 1/8 × 35 in.
Museum purchase, 1995 General Obligation Bonds (1998.20.28).

For students from the United States, Mexico presented opportunities for discovery. José Clemente Orozco had died, but Diego Rivera and Frida Kahlo were still alive, and Rufino Tamayo was enjoying his first one-man gallery show. A professor took our class for a visit to sixteenth-century houses located behind the cathedral on the Zócalo, structures whose owners were subsidized by the government to promote upkeep and maintenance. Such a federally subsidized program for preservation seemed visionary.

A university course in Mexican art history introduced me to colonial house museums in towns such as Pátzcuaro. Some of these homes had been left with original furnishings. I saw objects that turned out to be similar to those my wife and I later found in New Mexico: furniture of local woods, textiles and handspun cloth produced on colonial looms, utilitarian as well as decorative pottery, cazos (cauldrons) of copper (colonial traders from New Mexico returned with these prizes), wrought-iron pieces, metates and manos, and more (fig. 6), all identifiably Mexican. Religious art was plentiful in these settings. For three years, more or less, I was tempted to settle in Mexico for good.

< FIGURE 7
Alan and Shirley Minge, Albuquerque, 1951–52. Courtesy Ward Alan Minge.

Shirley's army assignment took her to Sandia Base outside Albuquerque in 1951. By now I was ready to return to the States; she had checked with the University of New Mexico to find, luckily, that it offered degrees in Latin American history. We were encouraged to enroll, and I was offered an assistantship toward a doctorate. We married on June 7, with the base chaplain presiding and teachers from the grade school next door as witnesses. We both started classes that fall semester.

We moved into a duplex at 217 Princeton Drive near Central and the University of New Mexico campus. I had no car after I surrendered the aging jeep to my dad in Denver. (He gave it to the Denver police, who used it for hauling floats in city parades.) We walked most places in Albuquerque, or went by bus. A neighborhood grocer was two blocks west, and a barbershop was located nearby on Central Avenue. Otherwise, our time was spent at the university or Sandia Base.

Our "ashcan neighbors" (Nora and Lawrence Dixon's description of our relationship) broke this routine by driving us around New Mexico, getting us acquainted with this great state. To return this generosity I cared for their side of the duplex when they traveled to California, Lawrence's uncle Maynard Dixon's country, or to the southern states where Nora had family. At home Nora occasionally urged me to buy Maynard Dixon's paintings, of which there were some stored in the basement in addition to those hanging around the house (Maynard Dixon's brother, Lawrence's father, had passed away, and I could have had any one of these for $25). Concentrating on New Mexican western paintings seemed way out of context.

The Dixon excursions found us in villages reminiscent of Mexico. Tradition appeared very strong. In northern towns like Mora and Chacon, Taos, Truchas, Trampas, Córdova, and Chimayó, many buildings were mudded. When we stopped for gas one Sunday in Galisteo, the attendant complained he could not save enough money for a trip to California. He owed a big debt to Ortiz y Davis, the owner of the gas station living next door in the family hacienda, where Ortiz y Davis also operated the local bar in one of its many rooms.

FIGURE 8
Tony Garcia, 2013. Courtesy Joe McKinney.

Soon the Dixons introduced us to the world of collecting in New Mexico. Nora collected Victorian art glass and belonged to an Albuquerque glass club; Dixon (everyone used his family name) was into guns. Albuquerque had no antique shops until the late 1950s, so collectors foraged junkyards and secondhand stores. The Salvation Army and Goodwill offered slim pickings, according to the Dixons, who knew the best sources. Visiting dealers who worked out of their homes was better. Yard sales had not caught on, but auctions were popular. Max Hood operated an auction house just east of the UNM campus on Central Avenue near Nob Hill.

On Saturdays we often went antiquing. Dixon drove the car while chain smoking roll-your-own Bull Durhams. One afternoon we stopped to see Tony Garcia and his wife, Minnie, who lived on First Street, just north of Central Avenue. Their rented house had been part of Albuquerque's fashionable "New Town," within walking distance of the Alvarado Hotel. Building parts filled both front and back yards. Minnie offered glasses of sun tea. Dixon had bought numerous antique guns here and Nora much Victorian glass. We learned that Tony scoured the country and seldom returned without a truckload of finds, mostly of Victorian vintage. While searching through a stack of doors I discovered one that was a slab of wood made to swing on pintles. Covered with visible marks made by an adz, it was obviously very old. In yet another stack of furniture were several *bancos* (benches) and *tarimas* (adzed planks on legs), all of pine, about two *varas* or just under six feet long. Dixon bought a bench and so did I, along with a couple of doors. Tony delivered these to our duplex on Princeton. This was the beginning of many years of collecting from Tony and our everlasting friendships with Tony and Minnie (figs. 8 and 9).

Tony was pleased that I bought the old door, confessing at the time that his only steady customer had been Santa Fe curator E. Boyd, purchasing on behalf of the Spanish Colonial Arts Society. But E. Boyd was ever short of funds. Being assured that I was

FIGURE 9
Minnie Garcia, 1992. Courtesy Ward Alan Minge.

interested in New Mexican colonial items, Tony bought more, objects he had often passed over for lack of customers. He half-jokingly called himself a coyote, a person combing the country for antiques. In reality he knew he was a dealer's dealer.

Around 1952, not long after meeting the Garcias, Nora spotted an ad in the local newspaper for "one of the last old adobe houses in New Mexico." In need of repairs, the house was mud plastered and could be had for a very reasonable offer, in a country setting in Corrales. But where was Corrales? Naturally, the Dixons knew.

Dixon drove us to Corrales the following Saturday, with car windows down and his ever-present Bull Durham roll-your-own tobacco pouch and papers. How to find the casa where there were no street names or numbered houses? We drove Alameda Boulevard west and over the single-lane iron Rio Grande bridge. Shortly the road made a turn north. There was no Coors Boulevard, only a trail where locals dumped trash or "made out," as we later learned. Stopping midway through the village at a country store on the east side of Corrales Road near Perea's Bar, we met the proprietors of the property we were interested in seeing. They led us farther north to an unpaved country road going west to a plaza with large cottonwoods, old San Ysidro Church (fig. 10), and the cemetery. Three large dwellings were on the plaza: the Bruna Gutiérrez Sandoval place with cement plaster on the east side, several orchards and the ancient mud-plastered Griego casa to the south and west of the church, and to the west the cemetery and the Clay G. "Red" and Inés Candelaria Gurulé (she descended from the Gutiérrez family) adobe facing the Sandovals across the road. The last turned out to be the object described in the ad Nora had seen. Behind a large *chabacano* (apricot) tree and remnants of a grape arbor stood a modest, run-down adobe, with no other buildings visible either to the south or west over the west mesa (fig. 12). The casa seemed enchanting and very possibly within reach. Even before inspecting the inside, we decided then and there to buy it.

FIGURE 10
San Ysidro Church, 1970. Courtesy Ward Alan Minge.

At the time, the Berry family, Seventh Day Adventists, lived in the casa as renters. Mr. Berry worked as a lumberjack in the Jemez Mountains, which accounted for the back acreage being cluttered with piles of lumber, a truck, and vehicle parts. Mrs. Berry guided us around, and we saw much disrepair and considered one or two rooms unlivable. There were six rooms divided by an ample hallway, and an outhouse but no plumbing. Four rooms had electricity, with cloth-covered wires looping from vigas and bare lightbulbs suspended in the center of the ceiling. An ancient well was worked by hand pump; the water was delicious. What is now the dining room was being used as a bedroom, while directly across the hall was a parlor heated with a cast-iron stove. The Berrys' kitchen was west of the parlor and had a door to the north, opening onto a path leading to the outhouse and clotheslines west of the house. A room west of the kitchen was a recent addition, possibly dating to the 1920s. It was built using *terrones* (sod bricks), which we learned were more substantial than adobe bricks (according to neighbor Rosaura Gutiérrez, who had lived there during the first years of her marriage, starting around 1900). Walls and part of the ceiling were collapsed. The floor appeared to be the original packed earth. An unused room farther to the south had an unusually large doorway, perhaps leading into a larger space. As it was a more modest room, it too was likely added, but sometime before the terrón bedroom. Rosaura told us that this room had been occupied by an aging Gutiérrez aunt who eventually died there.

Because of our excitement over this "sleeper," we gave little thought to the time, effort, and money needed for the problem at hand. Had I had any real notion of how many tons of adobe I would lift, along with additional tons of mud plaster, we might have thought longer and harder about a future here. My dad, however, helped with financing the property, which included nearly three acres and extended west to the acequia (irrigation ditch). We thought it was a bargain. The above took place in 1952. To secure the purchase required much paperwork, which turned out to be somewhat mysterious. We were told the Sandoval County land and water records had burned along with the courthouse in 1925. Officials handling titles explained that title clearances and insurance were available but that titles contained skimpy descriptions and only rude history.

We made the down payment and bought a used Ford station wagon. We could now commute into Corrales, and I was eager to start restoration. The purchase became final with an insured title and "clean" paperwork on February 27, 1954. A crumbling six-room adobe dwelling and 2.48 acres, more or less, became ours for the whole sum of $5,000. We heard sometime later that locals believed we had been taken for a ride. We thought we were being sensible at the time. The Cold War was ongoing, and the whole country was being encouraged to build bomb shelters. We rationalized that by moving to the country we could survive most threats. Our well had plenty of water, the irrigation ditch had more, and the acreage would produce food. We could renovate the adobe and furnish it with colonial New Mexican furnishings. And we could afford to do this while still in school. Shirley began to respect thick adobe walls.

FIGURE 11
Upper kitchen, 2012. Photograph by David Nufer.

Assuring ourselves that we had not blundered, I set to work virtually rebuilding much of the casa. I reroofed the existing rooms, supplied the well with an electric pump, and started accumulating building elements from 1952 through the summer of 1954. The Berrys cleared the indoors and backyard, where I began to find remnants of older foundations. Old stones lined bases of past rooms, and plantings appeared to grow along a building or buildings long gone. The Spanish lace vine that grew up the west wall of the west wing was one such plant. Unfortunately, I took few photos at the time. Preservation as a concept was little understood or encouraged formally in those days.

For those two years we commuted on weekends from the duplex on Princeton. While reroofing, I could not resist laying up walls. We had decided to wall in the area on the southeast to connect the two bedrooms, all of which eventually became the upper and lower kitchen and dining room (figs. 11 and 12). I obtained some adobe bricks and one sunny afternoon hoed a pile of mud and began laying them. The wall went up fast, since the bricks were large and the process was similar to laying up shaped stones. The following weekend I discovered that the wall had sagged and leaned way off center. I was surprised it had not toppled; I began dismantling, saving the bricks to begin all over again. About this time our neighbor, Mr. Griego, dropped by to give me encouragement and explained about working with a level and string. Miguel Griego and family became friends. They lived in the large adobe to the south of the cemetery, which once had a courtyard but now consisted of the east wing only. I felt sure it dated back to the eighteenth century.

FIGURE 12
Lower kitchen under construction, 1954. Courtesy Ward Alan Minge.

I started over with Señor Griego's instructions, placing the bricks (weighing thirty-four to forty pounds each) on the corners, going up three or four high while tapping the corners into true vertical indicated by a level. With a carpenter's twine stretched from one corner to the next, I placed several rows of bricks, and a wall began to take shape. Señor Griego cautioned against laying more than four or five rows before allowing the mud to dry. I started to mix mud (used as mortar) in a tub but learned the proper way to mix a large amount was to create a mixing hole in the ground. These simple basics began my career in restoring the walls of the casa over the next twenty years.

This same year I moved to another level in adobe construction: creating the corner fogón (fireplace) (fig. 13). That fall an Indian lady from the Pueblo of Santa Ana built the fireplace now seen in the guest bedroom, which had been the Berrys' kitchen. Casey and John Adair, who with their family occupied the north wing of the old Sandoval (Gutiérrez) house across the plaza, recommended her. She had constructed several traditional fireplaces for them.

> FIGURE 13
Fogón in lower kitchen, 2012. Photograph by David Nufer.

The elderly Indian lady appeared in October with an array of oddly shaped adobe bricks she had made. She took a saw to that corner of the floor, clearing a space where she began laying regular adobes in mud to form a base for the fireplace. This became the hearth. Upon the base she fitted two oblong adobes into channels she chopped into the walls and mudded, these going up the walls on each side of the corner. These "loaves" were about twenty inches long and six to eight inches thick. On their ends, she placed a large horseshoe-shaped brick of the same thickness to create an arched opening. We were fascinated, watching until she disappeared after lunch. A few weeks later she appeared on a clear warm day, this time with numerous wafer-like adobe bricks intended to form the chimney. These she affixed with mud into channeling up the wall, which was two inches deep. Meantime, the framing had dried, allowing her to mud in and sculpt the fireplace and mantel as it stands today. To finish her job, she climbed to the roof, where she created an opening for the wafer bricks to continue up the roof line about two feet. Once all this was sealed, and because her work below had not dried, she lit newspapers in the arched opening, where the smoke disappeared up the chimney. Adding some faggots for a real fire, we all watched as the wet adobe steamed while drying. As I recall, she asked for thirty or forty dollars for her work, along with a lunch or two. We used this fireplace frequently.

That same summer, while reworking the earthen roofs, I found that some were topped with as much as two feet of dirt, while the roof over the bedroom on the south had almost three feet toward one side. Not only was the excessive weight causing vigas to sag—one or two had ominous cracks—but also dirt was sifting onto everything. Removing all this dirt revealed traditional roofing methods, and from neighbors I learned how to prevent sifting dirt and leaks. If we decided to keep the dirt and mudded flat roofing, we should cover the decking of *latillas*, and over this a layer of ninety-pound tar paper, and then return the dirt and mud. Chamisa is a type of shrub growing around the casa, in the cemetery, and out toward the west mesa. Its stems grow tough, in straw-like clumps, and the old-timers believed that inserting chamisa above the latillas discouraged bugs and spiders. To complete the job, mud covered by

dirt was sloped toward the drains. Some wet springs, I later learned, caused a garden of weeds to grow on each roof. All these areas had to be kept clean, and especially so for easy removal of winter snows.

I had not yet finished with the roofing when the army decided to move us from the duplex on Princeton. Not only did the army move the household but also a truckload of architectural elements we had collected. The enormous van arrived at our casa Thanksgiving week on a cold, rainy day. Water dripped into the unroofed rooms, while those secured began to fill with furniture, beds, and all the rest. The worried movers invited us to stay in the van where we would be dry and safe, but we chose to keep to our own beds in our own casa.

Among items moved were eighteenth-century corbels from the Tomé church south of Albuquerque, a major undertaking. They numbered around forty, were each over six feet in length, and were quite large and heavy. We had stored some of them in our small basement on Princeton and others in a sympathetic neighbor's garage. The move also included old doors, windows, and some New Mexican furniture, along with electrical appliances lent by my anthropology professor, Florence Hawley Ellis. Our beginnings were an overwhelming mess and primitive to boot.

Meanwhile, our dear friend Mitzi Zoske Brady fantasized about our "hacienda" while all this was happening. She must have imagined we were luxuriating in a setting that included courtyards, arcades, corrals, fountains, and a large tiled kitchen, in short, those settings she recalled from staying at the Alvarado Hotel or from reading D.H. Lawrence's *Plumed Serpent*. She had retired from owning an antique shop in downtown Chicago and had opened Albuquerque's first such shop in Old Town, where we met her. She had been raised on White River near the Rosebud Reservation, South Dakota, where her folks had set up ranching after traveling from Minnesota by wagon when she was only six. Her experiences there were followed by colorful careers in New York, Chicago, and now, New Mexico. She sold only the finest and was admired by many for her impeccable taste and especially for her conversations and stories. She described herself as "bookish." She had been involved with literary movements in Chicago,

FIGURE 14
Parlor, 2012. Photograph by David Nufer.

which caught the attention of H. L. Mencken, with whom she corresponded.

The front parlor became our living quarters the first weeks in Corrales (fig. 14). We adapted Professor Ellis's appliances to the light socket. Late one Sunday morning while we were preparing breakfast (doubtless served on the bed) friends knocked at the front door, and among them was our Mitzi. Her curiosity would not be deflected. After her hilarity upon discovering our true conditions, we ate omelets and coffee and did the "grand" tour. Everyone was very polite and said they could see great potential in our future.

Reaction from our parents was more circumspect. My dad nodded his head and thought it a great investment. Aunt Augusta, Dad's sister, wept openly, thinking we were in hard times. Shirley often quoted her mother's reaction: "Well, if that's what you kids like!" But her dad, he just laughed and laughed.

CHAPTER 2

ADDING TO CASA AS THE COLLECTIONS GROW: NORTH AND SOUTH WINGS

< DETAIL OF FIG. 55
Weaving room, east end, 2012. Photograph by David Nufer.

AS CASA BECAME LIVABLE, WE ENCOUNTERED OUR FIRST PROBLEM: our collection of books. We agreed on a library entirely separated from existing rooms and possible future additions. It would be placed south of the existing structure over a lane formed by locals for taking trash to the rear of the property; neither the Berrys nor the Candelarias objected, and the dumping had gone on for some years. Pete Smith, our friend who constructed the library, placed the foundations directly over the road. Barricades were constructed to prevent trespassing and accidents.

After the Berrys' lumber and old cars were removed, and during preparations for the library around 1952–54, we exposed what appeared to be old foundation stones. They formed straight lines in places, and plantings indicated there had been a compound or buildings around a compound (fig. 15). The discovery, in turn, inspired thoughts of building a south wing. We had acquired a magnificent old loom, and experience in Mexico gave me the urge to include a gatekeeper's room. A chapel and master bedroom would compose a north wing extending into a west wing to enclose a plazuela (patio). The west wing would include a zaguán (entrance) and a *gran sala* (parlor) to incorporate our collection of eighteenth-century corbels. Made aware of these plans, Pete suggested pouring cement foundations for the entire structure while pouring those for the library. His idea was to create two-foot-square concrete slabs

FIGURE 15
Builder Pete Smith near exposed historic foundation stones at the southwestern corner of the Gutiérrez House, 1950s. Courtesy Ward Alan Minge.

with five one-inch steel rods to support the planned thick walls, which would never stand in water.

The accumulated architectural elements determined the shape and dimensions of the library. Tony Garcia found ancient hand-squared and beaded vigas (roof beams) on a ranch near Casa Blanca and the Pueblo of Laguna. They were over twenty feet long, or some seven or eight varas, and about eight inches square. George Pearl, an Albuquerque architect and longtime friend and supporter of the project, presented the doorway, a Federal-style structure with original glass panes, all of which determined the room's height. He had rescued it while working on an abandoned Luna family adobe casa in Los Lunas. Tony also turned up the fireplace mantel found in Coyote, New Mexico, and a wall cupboard known locally as an *alacena*. It was found in Ranchos de Taos, in an eighteenth-century adobe mostly in ruins. The cupboard had the original finish (a water-soluble brown paint), drawknife and adz marks, and no nails. The wrought-iron hinges and latch appeared to have been made locally. I had to stabilize the parts and framing with twine to fit the assembly into the library wall and anchor it in place before removing the twine.

In 1955 and 1956 we had the opportunity to purchase an abundance of colonial building parts. Our friend the historian Robert Delaney had met the Padillas, who were living on a ranch near San Pedro, New Mexico, and who wanted to sell a number of deserted adobe buildings they owned at that place. At Delaney's urging, Shirley and I drove old Highway 85 to find the ghost town and to meet the Padillas. They were surprised and pleased to learn of our interest and our intent to preserve what was salvageable.

Señora Padilla liked Shirley and straightaway invited her to the ranch house, where she produced some jerky and proceeded to break the pieces with a hammer, as one of the steps, she explained, involved in making a stew for lunch. Meanwhile, Señora Padilla walked me through eight buildings they owned: one, two, or three rooms each except the main structure attached to the church. For all this they wanted $150.

The church itself had an extraordinary ceiling, beautifully composed of pine vigas with hundreds of straight latillas spanning them. Padilla thought the parish still owned the building. Most members lived in Socorro, New Mexico, more or less across the Rio

FIGURE 16
Kitchen portal facing north portal, 1984. Photograph by Robert Reck.

Grande, and he would check into the parish's opinions on selling. We corresponded until that Easter, when he wrote that the parish had decided against it. During a visit a few years following, we found the ceiling had collapsed and had been covered in dirt and mud.

Most ceilings in the ghost town were traditional, seemingly very old large cottonwood or pine vigas, countless latillas, all very straight and finished with adz or drawknife. In the end we salvaged a dozen rooms, the wooden parts at least, and a chapel. I enlisted the help of a crew of air force historians from the office where I worked, but we couldn't save the adobe bricks, which broke no matter how carefully we pried them. Dr. Del Trester and Warren Greene helped in this dismantling, which required several weekends, while Pete Smith trucked the materials to Corrales.

By now stacks of vigas, latillas, window frames, and antique doors covered the backyard. With this abundance I pieced together the first segment of the kitchen portal (fig. 16). Squared cottonwood vigas from San Pedro made substantial supports; cottonwood

FIGURE 17
Valdez family, Velarde, New Mexico. Harinero, early nineteenth century. Gift of Ward Alan and Shirley Jolly Minge (1997.51.123).

vigas and latillas made the ceiling. While putting it all together I conceived of the idea of building a buttress on the southwest corner of the kitchen, which would support the portal ceiling while reinforcing that corner of the original house. I carefully arranged for an opening over a fledgling elm, because Shirley could not bear to destroy a tree. At that point there stood another elm to the west, roughly where the west wing was laid out. In the front yard, so to speak, there was an enormous apricot tree of the Old World type, yielding small flavorful fruit. A little to the east of it grew a small collection of vines, seemingly quite old, yeilding green, roseate, and black grapes.

Tony Garcia continued making great finds. He dropped by one spring day in 1959 with a large red *harinero* (grain chest) (fig. 17). We moved it into the kitchen portal, where it stood for years. During this same year, he located the eighteenth-century loom (according to its owners, who lived in the Española, New Mexico, area, it had been in use since about 1775), complete with five reeds and a tool chest. Word spread of its rarity, and subsequently a scholar from the Smithsonian came to examine and study it. She had studied looms from all ages. On a second occasion, I received a call from the director of the Columbus exhibition that the Smithsonian was assembling, "desperate" to locate a reed for a loom in the exhibit. He had been searching the country until a contact in Santa Fe suggested that if one survived, Alan Minge would surely have it. "Okay. You want coarse, medium, or fine?" I said. "I'll be right down," was his reply.

I spent that fall and the following spring extending the kitchen portal along the east face of the library. Pete Smith had extended the south library wall to the east, and in this section I placed the ancient, small *sambullo* (pintle) window. One could see Casa Griego from it. The casa was a popular subject for photographers, and residents there could watch processions to the camposanto. One day a crew member on our site asked Pete about the religious cult we must belong to, because his mother noticed that we burned candles at night—not realizing we had no electric lights at the time.

Through such happenstance, we became better acquainted with members of this long-established community. Before the move from Albuquerque, our neighborhood grocers, the Burtons, heard of our pending move and offered us a peacock and a peahen. The Burtons lived south of town. They were moving into Albuquerque and hoped we might give the birds a home at our place. The offer brought to mind palatial mansions in Mexico City, out beyond Chapultepec Park, where I had seen such exotic birds roaming in rose gardens. Of course, we would be happy to give them a proper home!

We set up an enclosure, but Shirley became distressed as Solomon broke tail feathers on the wires. She wrote zoos for information on the care and feeding of peafowl. Burton had explained how in a new environment they needed to be guarded in a pen for a month or so. The Brooklyn Zoo sent a mimeographed brochure explaining that once loose they would graze far and wide but return to roost in tall trees. Jezebel would likely nest in hiding during spring, until her eggs hatched. Young males matured in two years, and meanwhile, during the first year, would emit guttural moans if startled, particularly at night.

>FIGURE 18
Chapel, 2016. Photograph by Nora Vanesky.

True to form, Jezebel disappeared the following spring. One evening in June, Cleofás Griego herded her and three chicks toward our casa, flipping her apron and shooing them on. Those days both Solomon and Jezebel roosted high in the old cottonwoods fronting the Griegos' property. The Griegos didn't mind their screams. The chicks, all male, preferred the cottonwoods on the plaza. Toward that fall their moaning at night became indescribable.

One morning when the library walls were half completed we left for Albuquerque at the usual early hour and spied a pine box at the entry to the camposanto. A burial would take place that day. That afternoon Pete flagged us down at Perea's Bar. Inside, three customers connected us to the peafowl. They explained that they had started to dig the grave when they heard loud moans. They dropped everything and got away fast.

I reconstructed the small chapel from San Pedro by March 1962. Its dimensions and salvaged parts (pine vigas and latillas—the last stained red, yellow, and green) fitted perfectly into the south wing. I continued to use Spanish measurements throughout. As the walls went up I laid adobes in a pyramidal fashion, re-creating a *nicho* (niche) as originally found in the left wall in San Pedro. Our San Antonio bulto occupied the niche from then on. The entry to the south remained open, framed by large, squared cottonwood beams resting on corbels from the mission in Tomé, New Mexico. The floor was dirt at this time, and the walls I covered with white gesso above a dado of Bajada red earth (fig. 18).

To connect the existing west bedroom to the chapel, I created a dressing room/closet. Here in the south wall and facing onto the plazuela I placed a colonial window complete with original framing and sambullo, or wooden pintle hinges. Carved paneling made this window a special treat and rarity. Of particular interest to professors and architectural students from the University of New Mexico was the discovery of how this method of construction allowed the weight of the adobe wall to secure colonial doors, windows, and wall cupboards in place. Tony and I believed this special window to be one of the finest New Mexican colonial fixtures, but neither of us can recall its origin.

The chapel gained a tower after Tony located the appropriate bell (see fig. 44). A dealer found it while scouting ranches in northern Mexico. We felt uneasy about the bell because imports of antiques from Mexico were uncommon during the 1950s and 1960s; the exception was the Fred Harvey Indian Building shop in the Alvarado Hotel. Curiously, a metal cross applied on a side of the bell corresponded to the two metal crosses Tony brought to the collections from Trampas, New Mexico. E. Boyd, with the Museum of International Folk Art in Santa Fe, believed these to date back to the mid-eighteenth century and very possibly original to the mission at Trampas, dating from 1760. She had run across a reference to a blacksmith living there at that time. Master *santero* Horacio Valdez became fascinated with the bell and climbed a ladder several times to study it and to take photographs.

Once rooms were finished, I began using colored earth exclusively on walls, along with traditional gesso. I had been finding that Hispanos and Pueblo Indians used bright earthen colors that they applied mixed with water, much as a calcimine is used. A fine example could be found on the bright pink dado used in the nave of the Acoma mission. I had initially believed it to be commercial paint! And to pique my interests further, Miguel Griego showed me a deposit of light adobe-colored earth west of our casa and beyond the acequia; he claimed it had been used on walls in Corrales for generations.

My first attempt at mud finishing was in the upper and lower kitchen. I applied the slip with a brush, using a solution of Corrales clay mixed in a coffee can with water. The solution went on smoothly and produced a warm, earthy tone. For the dining room, I used a pink (but not that from Acoma), and after a year the walls turned a rusty brown. Acoma friends appeared one day with a flour sack of soft, pink stones that dissolved easily in water. The solution was quite dense, and a small amount covered many square feet—a supply to last many years. To clean surfaces while covering blemishes or small cracks, one needed just a small amount of pink stone dissolved in a coffee can with water and a paint brush. The Acomas were pleased with this but hoped that one day I would use the pink in the chapel.

The casa's family parlor received the strongest color from my growing collection of earthen samples. This included a Placitas yellow and gold, Dripping Springs green, a Cuba mauve, and Bajada red. There were others, including blues, but Bajada red seemed best in a Victorian parlor. Museum contacts in Santa Fe were intrigued but skeptical, until renovations to the Palace of the Governors revealed Bajada red under layers of other finishes used in its entry, dating to the eighteenth century or earlier.

The gallery and guest bedroom next to the parlor received Placitas earth. Hills surrounding that village abound in golds to bright yellow, whites, greens, and blue greens. I covered the gallery walls with off-white, while the guest room dado got Placitas gold with white gesso above the dado. The gold not only produced a durable surface but also allowed stenciling of birds just above the dado (fig. 19; see also fig. 20). The fireplace was covered with the same gold. Walls in the latest bedroom in the original dwelling ended with soft clay: Dripping Springs green. A box of this earth was given to me by Mrs. Walter K. Marmon, Laguna, who had used the same in her home at Dripping Springs where she had lived as a bride. Traveling to the site several miles south of the pueblo, I found the Marmon place, in ruins but on a hill covered with the same green soil and shale. The area was surrounded by mountains and valleys.

All rooms existing at the time of purchase were finally livable by 1960, including a kitchen and bath. We were employed, attending the university, and I had started a research project for the Pueblos of Jemez, Santa Ana, and Zia, commencing in 1955. At that time, I was the first historian hired to help the pueblos with their land and water claims. My work on this early case led to another contract in 1956–57, this time with the Pueblos of Acoma and Laguna. These commitments, along with Shirley's duties with the army, kept us away from the casa frequently.

On a summer evening Miguel Griego dropped by to caution that there had been reports of burglaries. He advised that we should start locking doors and hire someone to stay at the casa during the day. I told Shirley that we could place a table at the door with a bottle of wine and a five-dollar bill. She didn't buy it. Miguel knew of a Gutiérrez descendant, a direct descendant of Napoleón, who lived on the main road east and

FIGURE 19
Bedroom I, 2016. Photograph by David Nufer.

about a block away. This turned out to be Rosaura, who had been traveling daily into Albuquerque where she was working at a number of households as a cleaning lady. He was certain she would welcome the chance to work here in Corrales. José had died, and she had no Social Security or other income and was getting along in years.

Rosaura had married José, also a descendant of Napoleón, the last of that family to own acreage from the Rio Grande to an area west known as the ceja. Rosaura and José had spent their first married years at the casa, around 1900. She was still familiar with older parts of the casa. She knew how each room had been used and remembered all the plantings such as Seven Sisters roses, Spanish lace vines, traditional grapes out toward the plaza, and the apricot tree she had planted. She related how the families had called to each other across the plaza (front doors facing directly); she also told stories about the church, its masses and festivals, but mostly about family matters. The casa across the plaza belonged to Bruna Gutiérrez Sandoval, also a descendant of Napoleón; she was Rosaura's aunt. San Ysidro's annual festival was celebrated May 15, during which the priest blessed fields and irrigation ditches. With Rosaura's concurrence, we began using the name Casa San Ysidro, and the grand old apricot was known henceforward as "Rosaura."

Rosaura was at least seventy years old when she came to stay. She was tall and slender with thinning white hair and blue eyes; her left eye was blind. From the start she felt at home. Occasionally we found a dining chair facing the corner niche holding San José, her husband's patron saint. On one occasion we found her there praying her rosary. Once on returning home earlier than usual we found her with neighbor ladies giggling in the bathroom over a colorful clay Adam, Eve, and serpent in a tree that I had brought from Mexico. We became acquainted with Corrales through her. On the first Independence Day at Casa she came to tell us she received her first Social Security check, more money than she'd ever seen at one time. Could she take a vacation? She had always hoped to travel to Ojo Caliente, New Mexico, for the mineral waters and hot baths. Later that month she made the pilgrimage.

Upon reaching eighty, she decided to return permanently to her place on the Corrales main road. We waved driving past on summer evenings as she sat with relatives on the front porch. Early one morning the six-thirty news announced the death in a traffic accident of an elderly lady in Corrales, Rosaura Gutiérrez. She had crossed Corrales Road for mail and, in returning, had not seen the approaching auto.

< FIGURE 20
Tonita Roybal, San Ildefonso. Jar, 1910–25. Photograph by David Nufer. 8 5/8 × 9 3/8 in. Museum purchase, 1998 Government Obligation Bonds (1998.21.46).

CHAPTER 3

COMPLETING THE WEST WING: A MONUMENTAL TASK

CASA RECEIVED MANY GIFTS OVER THE YEARS, especially as the notion spread that objects there would be safe and protected forever, as some donors believed. Cleofás Griego dropped by one afternoon and was behaving rather strangely. I thought she did not want to visit. Rather, she settled for a stretch on a small chest near the front door and eventually left without a word. Later I discovered several old rosaries and a religious medal. The gift might have been connected to her family's conversion to Seventh Day Adventism, I surmised. I placed the objects in the chapel.

As with other items in the collections, they became part of the city's purchase in 1996. Included with these was Acoma's gift of paving stones. Tribal members wanted them to cover the sala and chapel floors. Other gifts included colonial handwrought keys, locally made tools of all sorts, textiles, metates, and manos. More unusual was a mortar and pestle (probably prehistoric) given to us by the master *carpintero* and santero Horacio Valdez. He and a friend were cleaning ditches near Ojo Caliente when a rainstorm sent them home. Returning later, they discovered that runoff had uncovered the stone pieces, in perfect shape and quite large. Horacio never tired of talking about old bells and locks. Both fascinated him.

Foundations for the west wing had been in place since the construction of the library. Now, however, I found the wing had to be built up simultaneously along with the north and south wings to interlock corners and furnish support for wooden elements. In the north wing, the master bedroom and bath were completed, along with that portion of the sala and west wing. This effort lasted throughout 1964 and 1965 (see fig. 15). Ceiling materials for the two rooms came from San Pedro, where the Padillas had sold us the buildings. The vigas and latillas were straight and beautifully finished by hand.

< FIGURE 21
North portal from the gran sala, looking east, ca. 1998. Photograph by Damian Andrus. Gift of Ward Alan and Shirley Jolly Minge (1997.51.146).

> FIGURE 22
Hispanic New Mexican or Isleta alacena/cupboard from Chical, early nineteenth century. Photograph by David Nufer. Gift of Ward Alan and Shirley Jolly Minge (1997.51.163).

The bedroom's blue moldings served as tie beams supporting heavy dirt roofing. Gracefully carved edges were the visible portion of large beams meant to prevent cracking in walls below while adding inter-est to the entire assemblage. Similar practices could be found in missions and village churches during colonial times, and we also used this style in the library. Pete Smith constructed windows and doorways to match those in Casa. I managed to build the fireplace and chimney as I finished roofing. The blue door leading into the bath came from the Loretto Convent in Santa Fe, which had been razed except for its chapel. Tony Garcia purchased a number of offerings after the convent was demolished and its contents sold to the public.

We got a second alacena in time to install it in the north wall near the fireplace. Tony had purchased this one in Chical on the Pueblo of Isleta reservation (fig. 22). I was experienced after installing one in the library, so I wrapped the pieces in twine and fitted the cupboard into place with little trouble. With the base of the alacena establishing the height of the dado, I lined the room lightly using a nail and level. I applied white gesso above, and below a mauve shade of earth found in deposits near Cuba, New Mexico. A geologist told me that such colors appeared near uranium deposits. A curator from the Metropolitan Museum of Art, during a visit, explained that Renaissance painters used a similar color.

It was a challenge to complete ceilings and firewalls (*pretiles*) on the north wing, erecting the lengthy portal to extend from the gallery along the south face of the wing and end at the sala. Tony found the dismantled portal, whose dimensions turned out to require no changes at Casa, where everything was measured in varas. The Isleta family of Jose Felipe Abeita had remodeled the family's ancient adobe and were willing to sell the portal, complete with corbels, uprights, and vigas, all worked by hand and obviously very old (fig. 23).

To say the least, assembly was tricky. I made special stone bases for each post and drilled holes into each base. Into these I inserted an inch of steel, and the posts did not move. However, to raise the posts, place the corbels, and arrange beams over these required extra hands. Luckily, help came from five Indians working our field

FIGURE 23
Abeita family portal at Isleta Pueblo, April 1936. Courtesy Ward Alan Minge.

next door. They took eagerly to a break, and in no time we had stabilized the framing. Now all in place, the portal revealed an unexpected conceit. The carpenter/architect had designed the posts and corbels to resemble a row of apple trees (fig. 23). The realization amazed the crew and me, especially when we contemplated the structure from across the plazuela. And lending the portal an architectural element of exceptional quality were the vigas and *tablas* (ceiling boards), finished by the builder using tools doubtless wrought by a local blacksmith. The Casa collections already included a number of these. From the front door an uninterrupted passage ran through the gallery, portal, and into the gran sala, stretching 140 feet. The bath and bedroom with portal were completed in 1965.

Our initial plan for a weaving room was to fill the middle section of the south wing from the library to the west wing, at this point an entrance into a gatekeeper's room. The weaving room would include the Española loom along with displays of early textiles. Plans changed after Tony Garcia turned up *trojas* (interior storage bins) found near Mora, New Mexico. Believed to be fairly common long ago, these items are now rare and seldom seen. They could be fitted along the south wall. Six-inch-thick planks, split and finished by adzing, formed two open bins roughly twenty inches or more, or two-thirds of a vara. The long plank, serving as an end for the bins, had to be anchored between walls, which seemed to offer the best security. So I constructed a partial wall extending into the room and mudded the plank. For storing precious grain or prepared flour, the set included a storage box fitted over the east bin and against the library wall. The entire assembly likely dated from 1800.

The *troja* was a meaningful addition to Casa, creating a working area for preparing and storing food for the kitchen. Now there existed two spaces in the room, and the loom would eventually occupy the west two-thirds. In the corner formed by the partial wall, I constructed another fireplace, this one with a stone base but otherwise with traditional adobe bricks shaped by hand. It heated the rooms better than expected, but a cast-iron stove kept us comfortable during the coldest nights and at Christmas.

As was the case with the north wing, the south wing adobes were interlocked, with the west wing wall going up simultaneously. Work on the south wing stopped during spring and summer, however, long enough to frame into place the zaguán leading from the plazuela through the west wing and into the corral. Architects and students of the Southwest were intrigued by the ingenious design and workmanship found in the materials of the structure. The corbels had been carved as one, with the viga across the opening facing the plazuela. The uprights supporting the two corbels held a gate that prevented large animals from entering the garden, while the other side of this gate was an opening for humans. Except for large doors immediately facing the corral, all the woodwork was hand hewn. The vigas were finished with beading made with a chisel; tablas were smoothed with a drawknife on the visible side, while the invisible top sides bore adz marks. Charles Welch, a graduate student at the University of New Mexico, built large wooden doors facing the corral, securing the planks with many wrought-iron nails. Their hinges and security bar are among the finest New Mexican iron pieces in the Casa collections.

FIGURE 24
West wing, west zaguán, and gran sala in progress, ca. 1965. Courtesy Ward Alan Minge.

We returned to the south wing during the summer of 1966 to work on the roof, doors, and windows. Again, Pete Smith made the windows to match existing paneling. The vigas for the weaving room came from an adobe schoolhouse in Belén, New Mexico, where they had been salvaged by architect George Pearl. We completed the south wing finally on September 4, 1966, and plastering followed in October and November.

Work on the two-story west wing had proceeded to accommodate construction on the north and south wings. Now came the arduous task of laying the adobes for the second floor (fig. 24). The gran sala measured roughly 40 × 20 × 20 feet. I determined that using a ladder instead of scaffolding would be the easiest approach. After a warm, clear day, I would return from town, mix mud in a hole, and carry a bucket of it up the ladder, followed by bricks, as needed, until darkness shut me down. I did most of this work with occasional help from Charles Welch. In May 1967, Shirley's cousin Charles Mullen arrived to help for part of that summer. At one point we tried to speculate on the number of adobes used thus far on Casa and could only imagine many thousands.

>FIGURE 25
Gran sala, 1984. Photograph by Robert Reck.

The gran sala was complicated, not just by its size but also because it would receive some of the earliest architectural components in the collections. Pete furnished framing, panels, and windows. I set into the walls, as they went up, two Acoma doors of the pintle type—one leading into the sala from the bath, and the second from the second-story bedroom leading onto a balcony (fig. 25). Architectural historian and

professor Bainbridge Bunting concurred with my belief that they were made in a shop located very early on top of the convent at Acoma. With the tribal governor's permission, we had located similar woodwork in the San Estevan church as well as in some of the private dwellings. We had been attempting to locate stone buildings possibly left over from before the destruction of the village in 1699 by Spanish soldiers. On another occasion I accompanied the Acoma governor, elders, and council officials on an inspection of the mission and convent roof, during which one of the elders pointed to an area on the roof, stating that it had been used by the Franciscans for teaching carpentry to Acoma boys. Framing for the doorway to the shop stood as a reminder, but the shop and other structures occupying the northeasterly corner on the very top of the convent were long gone. Recent tree ring dates from the convent timbers dated construction as beginning or ongoing in the 1640s.

In any case, the Acoma doors became part of the walls; their weight held them tightly in place. I found that with these doors and other pintle-hinged items, placing metal washers under the bottom point allowed doors to open and close smoothly. Three-fourths of the way up the south wall I installed an early window and balcony. Tony Garcia found the window in the Pueblo of Santa Ana. Two slabs form shutters and operate on pintles; the frame held mica at one time, or early glass. Tony also located the balcony, in a place north of the Pueblo of San Juan. The abovementioned Acoma door gave access to it.

The next step required great effort: placing the corbels and vigas over the entire wing. Only two pieces of bed molding, along with three dozen corbels, survived from the Tomé church ceiling (dating from 1738 to 1740 and remodeled in 1890). Above the bed molding (called "Franciscan cording") rested the corbels, of which only enough survived so that a single corbel could be placed at each end of a viga. They were shaped so that the heavy butt ends balanced on thick walls without support. A few retained numerals painted in black, no doubt signifying that they had been made in pairs. Too late I became aware that the shorter corbels—only six or seven survived—were meant to fit under the longer corbels and in this way extended support under the vigas and the

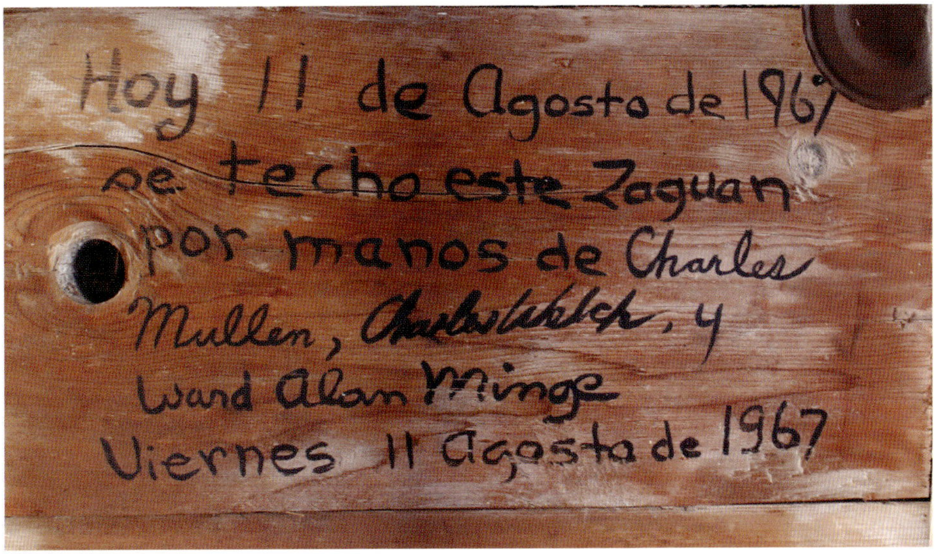

FIGURE 26
Signed tabla in sala, 2016. Photograph by Nora Vanesky.

dirt-laden roof. When viewed from below, the combination revealed opening pomegranate blossoms. I consulted with architects and structural engineers about raising the roof to complete this great ceiling with reproductions. The consensus was positive!

Charles Mullen, Shirley's cousin, helped me to get the corbels placed. We walked the vigas, one by one, up the north wall and each fitted perfectly on its corbels, which were quite secure. My dad, Martin, appeared during these activities and volunteered so that after the timbers were in place he spent a number of days nailing cedar tablas over the vigas. Charles, Dad, and I signed the ceiling tabla, July 22, 1967 (fig. 26). That night we danced around a bonfire behind the west wing, gradually feeding the flames with our very grimy clothes and underthings, while Shirley beat a Pueblo drum.

It was during that summer that the Pueblo of Acoma gave us enough paving stones to cover the chapel and gran sala floors. I hauled them from the quarry, where two Acoma men helped mine and load the pieces. Most were smooth and flat, varied in size and shape, and five to ten inches thick. In the course of that fall I rolled stones into place in both rooms, leveling each in sand while Shirley filled the interstices with

FIGURE 27
George Horace Long house, Ranchos de Taos, late eighteenth to early nineteenth century. Courtesy Ward Alan Minge.

bits and broken shards. Often into the morning hours she was helped by a mother cat and her three kittens.

The upper level in the west wing was finished with help from Charles Welch, who volunteered from time to time, but for this project he wanted pay. Over this we nearly came to a parting because of his poor work habits. Many afternoons I found him sleeping, which wasn't too distressing except that he'd slept most of the day or suffered over some unrelated distraction. With much prodding, the floor was eventually finished, so that, with windows and Acoma door in place, we had the west wing entirely closed in by the winter of 1967–68. We had planned a circular stairway to replicate that in the south tower at Acoma mission. The concept appealed to Welch, who shaped the pine steps by hand from logs whose ends were the same dimensions as an adobe brick. We were able to lay each step's end into the northwest wall/corner of the gatekeeper's room, as the wall went up over the cement base. Risers were separated on the opposite ends by circular pine pieces, thus mak-ing it appear that the steps were being held in place by a wooden column. In the years of use these steps never loosened. Considered unsafe or unwieldy, however, they were eventually replaced by an open stairway with a railing for easier entrance to the second floor.

The next architectural surprise came during the fall of 1970, when Tony Garcia appeared with zaguán doors out of the George Horace Long house near Taos, New Mexico (figs. 27 and 28). I had known of them several years earlier through Bainbridge Bunting, after he had discovered and photographed them in situ for an article. He described them to me as the finest in New Mexico. He thought they dated from the early 1800s, when Long supposedly built the house. However, Tony heard neighbors say the Long place had been a fort built by Spaniards during the eighteenth century. After the owner agreed to sell, Tony in his excitement drove immediately to Dixon, New Mexico, where he solicited Horacio Valdez's help in dismantling the zaguán doors.

The next day Tony drove the truckload to Corrales, and excitedly we determined where and how to fit these magnificent doors to Casa's facade. My dad helped to create a smaller, kitchen plazuela by enclosing the area in front of the library and portal as well as south of the upper and lower kitchens. I laid adobes over cement foundations and included two small rooms on each side, forming the opening leading to a large opening to fit the doors. The assemblage had all of its original framing. For the ceiling in the entry I used cottonwood vigas and latillas. The adobe firewall anchored the doors. Originally they included five hundred wrought-iron hinges similar to those found at the entry to the chapel at La Purísima Mission in California. And the heavy framing held rare iron fittings for a heavy crossbar. I had found a number of similar iron pieces and could not imagine their use until now. Impressive ironwork still existed in place on a small "people's door," which along with the rest are illustrated in Marc Simmons and Frank Turley's *Southwestern Colonial Ironwork*.

For a number of years Acoma friends Joe and Rose Ray encouraged me to install an *horno* (outdoor oven; fig. 28). We needed an horno for baking bread and other foods, to be authentically New Mexican. The Rays would start the project by making a model. Soon thereafter they appeared in the plazuela, where I was watering the garden and relaxing after having testified in Santa Fe for another Indian pueblo. "Come, come on Minge, see what we brought you," they laughed. I invited them for supper; Shirley was on an assignment with the army. "No, we have to go. Come see what's in

FIGURE 28

Zaguán portones from the George Horace Long house. Photograph by David Nufer.

the box." I dropped the hose and opened the box, which they had placed on the large grain chest under the portal. I carefully removed a complete, mudded model of the horno planned for Casa. In addition to a miniature adobe horno about ten inches high, there was a containing wall for ashes, a miniature Acoma water jar, a diminutive mop to clean the oven floor and for removing bread or other baked items such as fresh corn on the cob or a platter of chicken, a rag-covered stone doorway to hold the heat, another smaller stone to cover a vent atop the horno, and a neat stack of wood. Their grandchildren had helped put it all together and had built a fire in the oven for traces of smoke in all the right places. One look and I broke into tears. Joe came on to me with, "Minge, this is to make you happy!" But I was happy, very happy. We laughed at how the children had made it look like a real horno.

Now for the actual horno. One Sunday morning in July 1970 a pickup backed through the zaguán into the kitchen plazuela, where Joe and Rose unloaded boxes of shale stones, bags of ashes, and tools. They moved a stack of firewood I had along the south wall, leaving room for an horno. They traced an outline for the base, in which was included a low wall leading to the closed room. Base and wall would form a bin for discarded ashes. That first visit saw the base completed, using some of the stones with adobe as a binder. Several weeks later they tamped wet ashes into the base's open space until the mass reached within four to six inches from the top of the base. Over the entire base they puddled rich mud for the floor.

In August and September, Joe and Rose worked on a circular wall, the oven, and its dome. After reaching two or more feet in height, they waited a week for this part to dry. The walls into the dome were six inches, roughly. They completed the dome by carefully fitting mud and stones sloping toward an opening, or flue, at the top. I've made two hornos since, one for the corral and another for a friend. In both cases I found that the last row of stones around the flue locked into place much as in a stone arch. During Joe and Rose's final visit to the horno, they covered it with finishing plaster and christened it with a fire, which, in turn, dried the horno, now ready for use. I've cooked many meals in it since.

In 1982, Tony Garcia found a pair of triple corbels. How they had been used he did not know, but it seemed likely they had been used on an opening of some sort. With that in mind, I built a gateway on the site of the old Gutiérrez pathway through the front yard. By using heavy timbers for framing an opening and to support the corbels and the considerable weight from the adobe arch, the structure became an entry from the plaza to the front door of Casa. The front door came from Manzano, New Mexico.

The arched gateway was two feet thick or more, and the corbels extended enough on both sides of the opening to allow some narrow roofing. One could stay here out of the rain or sun. Two rows of grapes, thought by Rosaura Gutiérrez to have been brought to New Mexico by Spanish settlers, grew inside the entry. Just in front of the entry stood a utility pole, with wires leading to more utility poles. Members of the European Trust for Historic Preservation, during their visit in 1996, expressed concern over the community allowing utility poles and wires to detract from the setting.

CHAPTER 4

THE CORRAL AND OUTBUILDINGS

THE INSPIRATION TO BUILD A CORRAL to extend out from the west wing centered on the stone barn, received in the 1950s as a gift from the Barela family of ranchers living near Manzano, New Mexico (fig. 29). Because Casa was heated by stoves and fireplaces, there was always a need for wood, and vendors were ready and willing to supply it. Among them were the Barela brothers, who eventually brought most of the supply, harvested from their eight hundred acres. I would pay them for a load, and they invariably invited Shirley and me to visit the ranch.

We found the Barelas' ranch while on a trip to Mountainair and the abandoned missions in the area. They were razing a stone barn, which Lorenzo Barela explained had been built by ancestors who brought the stone by wagon from the ruins at Quarai. During lunch they insisted on hauling the entire building to Corrales if we seriously wanted it. It took them around a month of weekends to spread a large area beyond the west wing with stones and the wooden elements that had been the loft.

After nearly fifteen years of fitting and mudding stones in place, the barn's walls reached their original height. Many evenings I would relax by puzzling over the array, trying to find enough square shapes for eight corners. The walls were double thick, requiring an eye for fitting the stones as snugly as possible. The floor was the bare ground while the loft, reached by ladder, had hand-hewn decking over original vigas. The Barelas continued to deliver wood as long as we lived at Casa. They would back a truck against the north corral wall and toss the pieces onto an enormous supply between the warehouse and stables. Lorenzo would ask especially if they might see the barn where "we played as kids."

< FIGURE 29
Barn from the Barela family near the Manzano Mountains. Photograph by David Nufer.

Before roofing the barn, we put up the corral walls, extending two hundred feet beyond the west wing. In the west end we included large double doors with heavy framing and appropriate ironwork. Frank Turley mounted the pintle doors and forged

> FIGURE 30
Escusado *from Socorro, ca. 1880. Photograph by David Nufer.*

all the iron pieces except for a large old metal bar that attached below the reinforcement bar. It was part of our collection.

Bob Duffner, a historian with the air force, helped to assemble the walls, two feet thick and nine feet tall, placed on a base of sand and loose rocks for drainage. And to keep moisture off the base the initial courses of adobe bricks had been treated with oil or asphalt, a method adopted by some adobe makers who advertised them as waterproof. We continued to lay up the walls with untreated adobes, and we planted cacti on top. My intention was not to finish plastering while we waited to incorporate *dispensas* (storerooms), a tack room, stables, a smithy, and a carpentry shop.

As the walls went up, and with help from neighbors over Thanksgiving, we finished the barn roofing and raised a large tie beam into place followed by tin covering and siding to close in the south and north gables. Following this, the adobe *dispensa* was completed in 1988 and connected the barn to the west wing. That same year Tony turned up a vintage outhouse, a two-holer for a child and adult, which he had located abandoned near Socorro, New Mexico (fig. 30). I cleared an area west of the barn, dug a fifteen-foot hole, lined it with discarded railway ties, and cleared the grounds for a garden. The outhouse was centered against the south wall and was approached by a pathway. A pole fence circled the space, which one entered through a trellis gateway under which was placed a waiting bench. The arbor was covered after a year or two with climbing roses transplanted from Rosaura's front yard. They were recognized locally as the Seven Sisters (las Siete Hermanas). A blackberry patch soon thrived on the eastern half of the garden, while on the west we raised vegetables and flowers. Over several summers I raised heritage plants from seeds furnished by Marc Simmons. As I recall, two types of wheat performed very well, and heritage-type cotton thrived—but I had planted too late in the season, and the pods did not mature completely.

The dispensa between the west wing and barn went up with comparative ease. Vigas from Governor Manuel Armijo's ranch house in Lemitar, New Mexico, a few miles north of Socorro, furnished the base for roofing, which was topped with tin. On the other hand, the log bunkhouse and cook shack west of the garden toward the

FIGURE 31
Teodoro Griego, bunkhouse and cook shack, ca. 1875. Photograph by David Nufer.

west end of the corral itself proved challenging for several reasons. I had never worked with or lived in log buildings. The logs were very large and heavy, especially those on the bottom of the four walls, but Jesús Mendosa, my helper from Mexico, offered to find extra help. Our third challenge came when attempting to make sense out of logs and timbers strewn over the back half of the corral, unmarked and unnumbered. I had purchased the *fuertes* ("forts," or log buildings) from Laura Engelbrecht, a descendant of the Griegos, who had inherited buildings and land around Silencio, New Mexico. She was eager to dispose of her cabins before "hippies" burned them. Negotiations took place in 1968–69 for three—a large two-room fuerte still standing, and two smaller cabins—which had been dismantled but seemed better for the space being allotted to them in the corral, presumably near where they would eventually stand (fig. 31).

My initial impulse was to sort the unmarked logs, starting with the base logs. These were identified by traces of earth and some worm damage. I had an exterminator soak them with chemicals guaranteed to destroy termites, dry rot, and unknown invaders forever. Jesús found help (Erasmo, Fausto, and Plato), and this august crew worked base logs into their proper place. The bunkhouse went up first; after mounting and dismounting logs it took four tries to gain a good fit. At last, on the fifth try the structure became quite stable. If the going got tough, the team accused one another of not eating enough beans for breakfast.

There was much to learn from the experience. Window and door openings proved helpful; in sorting the logs we found the various lengths that were created for these openings. After the largest logs were in place on the bottom, they were followed by somewhat lighter logs. The cabin's corners fitted or locked by half-moon or quarter-moon cuts to the beam ends. The former were used on the bunkhouse and the latter on the cook shack. Atop each wall a roofing log supported vigas, which in turn were anchored by roofing beams and gable parts formed of rough-cut timbers with bark on the exterior.

After only two adjustments to logs, the cook shack stood firm. Both fuertes received tin roofing, after which each received mud and stone chinking between logs. Jesús helped by mixing mud and straw for the floors, after which we added porches to the front of each. The cook shack we placed away from the corral's southwest corner, imagining that live-in *peones* could plant a garden or raise chickens here. A pole fence enclosed the area in which we placed a long, narrow, hollowed log used for feeding poultry. The Casa collections now included numerous such one-of-a-kind regionally made domestic items.

Among traditional plantings at Casa, I placed a *membrillo* (quince tree) outside the northwest corner of the main garden fence. Between the two cabins I planted peach trees, using pits received from a Hispano rancher near Las Vegas, New Mexico. We had peaches during the second summer because the sprouted trees grew phenomenally fast and produced white-fleshed fruit that visiting neighbors recognized for their sweetness. I had long been attracted to *garambullos* (black currants), which grew wild in old, established orchards near Casa. I was certain these berries had been introduced by early settlers. Two rows grew successfully along the road north of Casa, and there were several bushes in the plazuela as well. They were covered with yellow blossoms each spring, turning into black currants, which made great jam.

Across from the cook shack and on the far west wall next to the large gate, we built an adobe tack room. I had thought that if ever the compound opened to the

FIGURE 32
Stable under construction, 1989–90. Courtesy Ward Alan Minge.

public it might serve for admissions and gift shop. As one might have guessed, Casa had become more than our initial vision of a simple place to live. Here the walls were two feet thick, with a window facing into the corral and a door centered on the north wall. As with the existing outbuildings, the floor of the tack room was dirt, and it had a traditional ceiling and tin roof.

In the northwest corner of the corral I constructed a second horno. Tony Garcia had found a rare, wedge-shaped adobe mold, obviously used at one time for constructing hornos. As I recall, the project required around two hundred wedge-shaped bricks, which determined size and shape of the oven and dome. The final product sat on an adobe bench wide enough to hold tools and food during use.

Stables followed along the north wall of the corral (fig. 32). By now I was using old timbers and leftover odds and ends. I parked old wagons in stanchions (fig. 33); they held some harness, farm tools, and a traditional feed trough consisting of a hollowed cottonwood log fitted onto a pair of heavy wooden legs. Tony found one of

FIGURE 33
North Carolina Hackney wagon sold by the Ilfeld Company, late nineteenth century.
69 1/2 × 127 1/2 × 65 in.
Museum purchase, 1995 General Obligation Bonds (1998.26.44).

> FIGURE 34
Hispanic New Mexican arado/San Ysidro plow, before 1850. Photograph by David Nufer.
16 7/8 × 135 1/2 × 5 1/8 in.
Museum purchase, 1995 General Obligation Bonds (1998.27.6).

the wagons at the Pueblo of Laguna. It had seen little use and quite likely had been sent there to the resident farmer employed by the Indian agency in Albuquerque. The second wagon had been owned by a local Hispano family who no doubt used it for shopping, going to Mass, and as an all-purpose vehicle before the advent of the auto. A third wagon had belonged at one time to Manuel Martínez, brother of Padre Antonio José Martínez, historically renowned author and priest from the Taos area. On the back wall of the stables hung a rare San Ysidro plow and its tongue (fig. 34). The plow appeared to have been made by a carpenter using traditional design and dimensions, because I found plowshares that fitted and could be interchanged according to how they were to be used in the field. For years I had been unable to find a tongue, until one afternoon, driving into Tony Garcia's backyard, I saw a long slender pole standing against the old elm. I sensed what it had to be. There were holes at one end for securing to an ox yoke, and a slot at the other to secure the tongue to the plow. When I brought it to Casa, the tongue slipped easily and snugly onto the plow. The plow and tongue were no doubt rare survivors of many that had once been used on this frontier.

A most unusual post held poles to enclose one stanchion. It was some four varas (or eight to ten feet) high, with about three feet into the ground.

FIGURE 35
Blacksmith Gary Williams at the forge, 2012. Photograph by David Nufer.

FIGURE 36
Hispanic New Mexican and Mexican iron tools from the Minge Collection, eighteenth to nineteenth centuries. Photograph by Damian Andrus.

Tony found it in Paguate, a settlement on the Pueblo of Laguna. Its massive, sculptural qualities were part of the entrance to the Hispanic Southwest portion of the Boston Museum of Fine Arts bicentennial exhibition, which traveled the United States in 1975 and Europe the following year.

Farther along the north wall toward the west wing I had planned a carpentry and smithy facing the woodpile (figs. 35 and 36). A storage shed on this site was dismantled, along with the enormous woodpile, after the City of Albuquerque acquired the property. Both shops were combined into one building and were added at that time. Their design and furnishings were in harmony with Casa's outbuildings and were enjoyed by interested museum visitors. They were constructed with great care and sensitivity by Genaro Apodaca.

CHAPTER 5

CASA ROOMS AND FURNISHINGS

AS CASA'S COLLECTIONS EXPANDED, Shirley and I learned to live in colonial New Mexico. Fittingly and naturally the various rooms and outbuildings came together. I had used the colonial measurements, basically the vara (about thirty-three inches), for all dimensions in the rescued architectural elements so that furnishings appeared comfortably "at home." I was assured by museum professionals that their institutions paid dearly to achieve an equivalent of our climate with its low humidity. During our years at Casa we found no evidence of damage to textiles, manuscripts, or books. Nor was there ever a problem with mildew. We lived with and used rooms carefully; we were dedicated to preserving and protecting the collections we hoped revealed the unique cultural development on New Spain's northern frontier.

COCINA (KITCHEN)

Upper and lower sections of the kitchen were finished in a coating of earth found about one-quarter mile west of Casa. Our neighbor Miguel Griego introduced me to a low bluff where deposits of earth with a slight rose shade had been gathered by Corraleños for generations. At the site I found the ruts of aged wagon tracks. The tone was subtle, but with more life than the ordinary ditch mud used in making adobe bricks. The ceiling in the upper section was original to Casa and had a blue calcimine stain after years of roof leaks.

While initially reworking the original casa, I added ceiling walls and a fireplace to close in this section of the kitchen. I broke through the wall into the dining room, leaving sloping portions to serve as buttresses. The vigas added were from the nineteenth century, milled and planed. I removed a large amount of dirt from the upper roof, creating a pile under the upper kitchen window. There, we planted cacti and yucca dug at Coyote Canyon south of Roswell, New Mexico, before the location

< FIGURE 37
Hispanic New Mexican trastero collected near Alcalde, mid- to late eighteenth century. Photograph by Damian Andrus. Gift of Ward Alan and Shirley Jolly Minge (1997.51.2)

became a state park. The heavy beam supported by corbels dividing upper and lower kitchen was a mistake—artlessness caused by my inexperience. However, the beam created a sense of strength and security.

Professor Robert Delaney helped to lay the first bricks in the lower area. We found them in an arroyo north-northwest of what in those days was known as the University of Albuquerque (now St. Pius School). There had been a kiln nearby. We collected enough of these discards for the gallery floor and a small portion of the plazuela. After a few beers we used our eyes for levels, and our inexperience was obvious. I had constructed the fireplace applying techniques learned from the Santa Ana lady who made the fireplace in what we were now calling guest room I. The fireplace was completed by Christmas Eve 1954, and we celebrated our first fire, which warmed the entire kitchen and dining room (see fig. 13). Over time I was able to install the comal, an iron trivet, and two *asadores*—long spits that were leaned against the hearth while roasting meats. We enjoyed many meals using these utensils. The comal, a flat stone whose surface had been "cured" to fry everything from eggs to pork chops, was important enough for families to pass along in wills, and metal comales were especially prized, though few survived. We had a fire in this fireplace from November through March each year.

Tony Garcia purchased the blue woodstove used by the Ortega family in Chimayó, New Mexico (see fig. 11). Parts of it had been manufactured in Pueblo, Colorado, and I speculated that the stove had been shipped to Santa Fe around the turn of the century, delivered by the Denver and Rio Grande Railroad. I fancied that the Ortegas had purchased the stove in Santa Fe, taking it to Chimayó. I was explaining all this to a tour group, after which a tall, distinguished gentleman assured me that I was correct in my assumptions that his grandfather had bought the stove in Santa Fe and then driven it by wagon to their home, where he and his grandmother and other family members had used it through World War II, after which they remodeled the house.

A pantry served as entry from the kitchen portal into the upper kitchen. This small passage had been created by placing a wall through what had been the original kitchen as identified by Rosaura Gutiérrez. On the other side of the wall we made a bath. Ceilings over these rooms had unpeeled latillas and hand-finished vigas. The pantry, however small, held a refrigerator and a nineteenth-century cupboard made from old shoe crates by the Bernalillo, New Mexico, carpenter Carlos Sena, Tony Garcia's uncle.

One of New Mexico's finest *trasteros* (cupboards or armoires) stood on the south wall in the upper kitchen. Thought to be made in the mid-eighteenth century, painted a deep blue-green, and constructed without iron accessories, it appeared in numerous publications (fig. 37). It was also featured in color on page 114 in Lonn Taylor and Dessa Bokides's *New Mexico Furniture, 1600–1940*. During an *Antiques Roadshow* taing, the Keno brothers visited Casa and discussed the trastero's merits with Casa's late curator, Dr. Andrea Gillespie. Tony had found the piece on a ranch near Alcalde, New Mexico.

FIGURE 38
Higinio V. Gonzales. Tin frame, ca. 1860. Mexican painting, San Juan Nepomuceno, ca. 1835. 27 1/2 × 21 3/4 in. (overall). Photograph by David Nufer. Gift of Ward Alan and Shirley Jolly Minge (1997.51.18).

FIGURE 39
Hispanic New Mexican trastero collected in Monticello, early nineteenth century. Photograph by Damian Andrus. Gift of Ward Alan and Shirley Jolly Minge (1997.51.11).

COMEDOR (DINING ROOM)

The *comedor* had a second pine trastero (fig. 39), considered by some to be even finer than that in the kitchen. This was also shown in *New Mexico Furniture, 1600–1940* (page 106). It had metal half-pin hinges and a lock. The Keno brothers were impressed by the framing, paneling, and hand finishing throughout. I've wondered if the panels on the doors might be an attempt to render "linen fold" (wooden relief carving). The cupboard came from Monticello, New Mexico, and dated to 1800 or earlier.

I had hoped to plaster the comedor with pink earth. Acoma friends knew of this and brought a flour sack filled with it. My friends later told me the earth came from an ancient deposit. This beautiful pink, as with all earth colors used in Casa, can be cleaned and freshened as required by dissolving a bit of earth in water and washing the walls with the mixture.

Doubtless the unique acquisition in this room was the corner nicho shrine by Higinio V. Gonzales containing a bulto of San José (Saint Joseph; see frontispiece, p. 2). Lane Coulter and Maurice M. Dixon Jr. (*New Mexican Tinwork, 1840–1940*) found it to be one of the three largest works created by New Mexican tinsmiths (the other two were in the Casa collections as well). The nicho also appears in Maurice Dixon's recent publication *The Artistic Odyssey of Higinio Gonzales: A Tinsmith and Poet in Territorial New Mexico*. Included in this book are discussions about dating, workshops, and New Mexico tin objects in general. Nearly three feet high and two feet wide, and constructed from tin containers, this work hangs by rawhide straps. Three-foot panels hold early glass with Moorish-style framing. The center panel makes up the door. Two birds on top appear to be eating cactus fruit. The structure, complicated and decorated with highlights of color, gives off a silver and golden sheen. The nicho was our first spectacular acquisition from Tony Garcia, who claimed to have found it in Chávez, New Mexico, south of Albuquerque. No doubt this amazing object inspired us to explore New Mexico's past. It entered the collection in 1953.

On the east wall stood a six-plank chest resting on a stand, both in excellent condition. At one time the chest had a lock, and for ornamentation, a distinctive overhanging on the lid, which was seldom found on early New Mexican chests. Scholars dated this chest to 1800 or earlier, the same period as the trastero.

The dining table, although small, was one of a kind, even in its day. The maker treated it as something special, with its hand-adzed but smoothed planking secured with costly wrought-iron nails. Stretchers were densely decorated with designs inspired by Indian motifs. The table was paired with a similar but more refined table from Spain in the exhibition *The American Craftsman and the European Tradition, 1620–1820*, held at the Minneapolis Institute of Arts, September 23 to December 31, 1989. A catalog of the exhibition discussed merits of both (plates 81 and 82, pages 200–201).

FIGURE 40
Hispanic New Mexican chest, early nineteenth century. Attributed to the Valdez family ofcarpenters, Velarde, New Mexico. Photograph by David Nufer. Gift of Ward Alan and Shirley Jolly Minge (1997.51.19).

GALERÍA (ENTRY HALL)

Called the galería, a narrow passageway came through the east wing and out into the plazuela. The ceiling had to be replaced, and I used milled and grooved vigas purchased from Tony Garcia before we moved to Casa. These may have misled researchers to date Casa to an origin estimated at around 1870. The surer way to date Casa is from vigas in the older sections that retain bark.

The galería exhibited several important pieces from the collections. As one entered the front door, there stood a small, elaborately carved box on legs dating to around 1800 and attributed by Lonn Taylor and Dessa Bokides to the Valdez family of carpenters in Velarde, New Mexico (fig. 40). On the wall above the chest hung a Mexican or Spanish mirror purchased at the Fred Harvey Indian Building at the Alvarado Hotel.

FIGURE 41
Hispanic New Mexican harinero from Arturo Borrego, El Guique, ca. 1690. 22 3/4 × 74 1/2 × 23 1/2 in. Photograph by David Nufer. Gift of Ward Alan and Shirley Jolly Minge (1997.51.15).

On the south side stood one of the older chests, with large dovetailing and lock and ring on the lid for lifting (fig. 41). Wear on the lid attested to great age, possibly eighteenth century or earlier. Preserved inside was the original divider, with the same adzed dimples in the wood as the unfinished interior of the box. Metal clasps reinforced the corners, and these had been fixed with wrought nails. Tony stated that he found the piece in El Guique, New Mexico, north of San Juan Pueblo (now Ohkay Owingeh), where he purchased it from Arturo Borrego. Tony also stated that some of the farms and ranches in this area were survivors from New Mexico's earliest settlements, beginning in 1598.

The galería further included a number of rare religious items as well as a tin chandelier hanging by a chain of coffee-can rings. Tony found it at Ranchitos, New Mexico, in what had been a dance hall. Above the large chest hangs one of the few church items (as opposed to laical use) in the collections, an enormous frame of many colors with two handles on the back for use in carrying the saint into the fields, along with the priest, on the saint's day. The frame enclosed a portrait of San Ysidro printed in either Mexico or Saint Louis, a romantic version and highly visible on May 15 (San Ysidro feast day). Farther along the south wall was a large painting of Our Lady of Guadalupe, also a church object, painted on canvas in Mexico around 1750. According to Tony Garcia, the seller explained that it had been removed from the Pueblo of Isleta mission to a chapel created by Isleta families in Chical. However, the parish eventually abandoned the chapel and its furnishings. The painting was in excellent condition, beautifully decorated with roses and cartouches, one showing the basilica of Our Lady of Guadalupe, north of Mexico City, as it appeared in the eighteenth century.

Along the north wall were sconces and retablos, religious depictions on canvas and wood. Near the parlor door was a painting on wood of San Acacio, patron of the military; his name is scratched in the lower right corner. The saint depicted here was particularly notable, wearing the Spanish uniform visible around New Mexico in 1800: a black Spanish hat, large blue coat with a red lining, leather chaps, and black shoes. Between the two bedrooms and on the wall hangs an early, fine example of Federal period tin framing with a Mexican painting of Saint John of Nepomuk. Lane Coulter and Maurice M. Dixon Jr., in *New Mexican Tinwork, 1840–1940*, described the frame as "one of the earliest examples of New Mexican tinwork" (see fig. 38).

LA SALA PARA LA FAMILIA (PARLOR)

One entered the parlor through a doorway and a remarkable door covered with moldings carved and laid in patterns along with carved paneling. We purchased the door in Chacon, New Mexico, while on a Sunday drive. A resident was selling several doors, all different, from his garage. We subsequently learned from Bainbridge Bunting that they were the work of a local carpenter, Aniceto Garduño. He had located Garduño in a census and found his grave next to a chapel in that place. One could spot Garduño's woodwork on some of Chacon's buildings and in Mora, New Mexico, down the valley.

The room was otherwise filled with Victorian furnishings inherited from the Minge and Jolly families. The walls were covered in a rich Bajada red clay, named after its source on La Bajada hill between Santa Fe and Albuquerque. On the west wall were ornate gilded sconces, likely made in Mexico. We had purchased these in the Alvarado Hotel's Fred Harvey Indian Building. Iron grillwork in the north window as well as the grilles in adjoining bedrooms came from windows in a defunct cantina in Anton Chico, New Mexico, where Tony Garcia was told Billy the Kid used to stop for refreshments. Made from wagon-wheel tread, they amazingly fit the casa openings after Marc Simmons and Frank Turley worked them over on their portable forge. Thieves had entered through one of the windows, but we had no such visitations after the grilles were installed (see fig. 14). For Christmas I often ornamented a small tree on a parlor table, as grandmother Minge would do in a German American community back in Kansas where my grandparents homesteaded shortly after the Civil War.

GUEST BEDROOM AND LIBRARY

We made the room next to the parlor into a guest room and library, with a single bed and shelves containing Shirley's collection of Civil War books. The renters had used the room as a kitchen, and with Pete Smith's help the shelves were redone for the books. I made the walls a gesso white above the Placitas gold earth of the dado. Rich gold clay abounds in the mountains around Placitas, New Mexico. Except for a viga, which had to be replaced, the ceiling was original to the casa as was the quite old and worn flooring. The pine furnishings were nineteenth-century New Mexican: a small bed from the Taos area, a table, and a desk. The bed was shown in Taylor and Bokides, *New Mexico Furniture, 1600–1940*, page 203, plate 203 (see fig. 19).

GUEST BEDROOM II

Through the last doorway on the north side of the gallery one entered a second bedroom (fig. 42). Its walls were of green earth, the earth coming from the Marmon ranch south of the Pueblo of Laguna. Mrs. Walter K. Marmon told us that as a bride she

FIGURE 42
Bedroom II, 2012. Photograph by David Nufer.

used the green to finish the inside of the ranch house at Dripping Springs. She invited me to visit the ranch and collect what I needed. I found the house in ruins on a hill of this remarkable green. The springs that gave the ranch its name produced water for the settlement in a semi-cave setting.

The former Gutiérrez owners added the room sometime after World War I using *terrones*. The ceiling had been covered with paper, but the vigas and decking were original. The door and transom were among architectural elements obtained in the Padilla purchase at San José. The ancient slab door in the east wall was among the first items we purchased from Tony Garcia when we met him initially on Albuquerque's First Street.

Here the furnishings were New Mexican pine of the nineteenth century: a wardrobe, chest of drawers, chair, bedside table, a most unusual bed, domed chest, and a cradle. The cradle was from Chacon, another example of Aniceto Garduño's

FIGURE 43
Aniceto Garduño, Cradle, New Mexican Empire style, ca. 1880. 20 1/2 × 35 × 31 1/8 in. Photograph by David Nufer. Museum purchase, 1995 General Obligation Bonds (1998.17.49).

carpentry (fig. 43). The chest of drawers and bed were reproduced in Taylor and Bokides, *New Mexico Furniture, 1600–1940*, page 195, plate 193 and page 202, plate 201, respectively.

EAST BATHROOM

Both the bathroom and the entry hallway to the kitchen formed the first kitchen of the Gutiérrez casa, according to Rosaura Gutiérrez. We needed to find space for a bath, so we had Pete Smith construct a partition to create the two areas and install plumbing, bath, lavatory, and toilet. The ceiling extending over both rooms was original, with bark-covered vigas.

Pete bricked in a tub purchased during an estate sale of contents from Monkbridge Manor, a former governor's residence on Fourth Street in Albuquerque. My father donated the lavatory, which he brought to us on a visit from Denver. Above this hung a large tin frame in which a mirror had replaced the saint originally in the frame. This item is pictured in Coulter and Dixon, *New Mexican Tinwork, 1840–1940*, page 98, figure 5.51. According to the authors it was one of the three largest New Mexico tin creations and under bright light made an unforgettable impression. At the entrance stood a small trastero purchased from Mitzi Zoske Brady's antique shop in Albuquerque's Old Town. The cupboard had belonged to a son of Barbara and Albert Simms. I had planned a small fireplace to be erected at the corner at the foot of the tub but never seemed to have the time to build it.

FIGURE 44
Bell tower with Mexican bell above oratorio, 1959. Courtesy Ward Alan Minge.

ORATORIO (CHAPEL)

A bell tower plainly visible from the plazuela topped the *oratorio*, and it was topped by a perfect bell purchased by Tony Garcia from an itinerant Mexican dealer (fig. 44). He claimed the bell came from a ranch near Mexico's northern border. Fascinated, Horatio Valdez—New Mexico's master santero climbed a ladder to study the cross overlaid on the bell's front side, which was identical in design to the two crosses from Trampas in the chapel. He believed, as did E. Boyd at the Museum of International Folk Art in Santa Fe, that the crosses had been forged by a local blacksmith in the mid-eighteenth century and very likely dated back to 1760, the year the mission had been completed. Discussion of the crosses, along with a photograph, appears in Simmons and Turley, *Southwestern Colonial Ironwork*, pages 166, 169, plate 9.

Upon leaving the gallery, one encountered the "open" oratorio (chapel) facing the plazuela from under the portal, an area only partially protected from the elements. Tony Garcia arrived one day with paneled double doors purchased from a family in

< FIGURE 45
Hispanic New Mexican doors to Duran family chapel, Talpa, early nineteenth century. 71 3/4 × 41 1/2 × 2 3/4 in. (closed). Photograph by David Nufer. Gift of Ward Alan and Shirley Jolly Minge (1997.51.147).

FIGURE 46
Hispanic New Mexican banco collected in Las Trampas, early nineteenth century. 27 1/2 × 50 1/2 × 16 1/2 in. Photograph by David Nufer. Museum purchase, 1995 Government Obligation Bonds (1998.18.17).

Talpa, New Mexico, who had owned a now-abandoned oratorio (fig. 45). The age of the doors was uncertain, but they appeared to be of a style popular in the early nineteenth century or earlier. The panels had traces of blue, yellow, and red paint, with flecks of what appeared to be dried blood. According to Tony, Penitente brothers had used the chapel as a morada (meeting house). I mounted the doors in an adobe wall to enclose the opening and discovered later that the corbels framing the new entry were similar to those in the chapel in Talpa. As with other doors mounted with pintle hinges in the collections, I placed washers under these, and they moved smoothly.

Other wooden parts in the oratorio came with the chapel we purchased, along with eight houses, in San José, New Mexico. A stepped niche in the west wall was copied from the original. We formed a stepped opening using modern adobe bricks, with no support other than mud for laying the bricks and for a plaster finish. San Antonio (Saint Anthony, patron of households) occupied this special place.

The stone floor was part of a much larger gift of paving stones from the Pueblo of Acoma. Tony found a prie-dieu, or kneeling bench, in Lemitar, New Mexico, where it had been in a chapel at one time. The two bancos, or benches, Tony purchased from members of a Penitente morada in Trampas, New Mexico, who understood that they had been pews in the church (fig. 46). One of these was illustrated and discussed in Taylor and Bokides, *New Mexico Furniture, 1600–1940*, page 84, plate 93.

FIGURE 47
José Rafael Aragón, Hispanic New Mexican retablo, San Ysidro Labrador, 1820–60. 17 3/4 × 12 1/4 × 1 in. Photograph by David Nufer. Museum purchase, 1995 Government Obligation Bonds (1998.18.35).

Bultos, retablos, and relics filled the oratorio in a brilliant array. However, we were never lucky in locating a small reredos (altar screen), and I had decided, meanwhile, to create one myself above the altar (see fig. 18). I dedicated the work to José Rafael Aragón, one of New Mexico's early master santeros. I studied photos and illustrations of Aragón's retablos, visiting those in the Santuario de Chimayó, New Mexico (fig. 47). My collection of earthen colors worked well on the white wall. My design allowed four of the larger retablos to occupy four vacant squares, two on each side of the crucifix by José Benito Ortega from San Miguel, New Mexico. On each side of the crucifix itself, I placed straw appliqué crosses to represent the thieves crucified with Christ. Tony found the adzed altar board, originally from a defunct chapel in the hills above the Pueblo of Cochiti, and I installed it over three adobe tables.

> FIGURE 48
Higinio V. Gonzales, Hispanic New Mexican processional cross and torches collected in Manzano, ca. 1875. 94 × 30 3/8 × 7 in. (overall). Photograph by David Nufer. Museum purchase, 1995 Government Obligation Bonds (1998.18.14-16).

Among the rarer religious items were two tin torches and a processional cross made by Higinio V. Gonzales, found in a church in Manzano, New Mexico (fig. 48). Coulter and Dixon dated the three to around 1875 and found them to be among the more impressive tinwork they had studied (*New Mexican Tinwork, 1840–1940*, see pages 36–37, 108–9, plates 4.81 and 5.67). The pieces also appear in Maurice Dixon's recent publication *The Artistic Odyssey of Higinio Gonzales: A Tinsmith and Poet in Territorial New Mexico*.

One of my favorite bultos was the youthful Christ teaching in the temple as rendered by Aragón. He holds a banner decorated with a lamb in the left hand, while the right hand is raised to emphasize a point in the lecture. The work is in excellent

condition, as if new, and stands in a glass case with a decorated wooden frame. The array stood on a shelf to the left of the oratorio entry, and beside it lay a human skull, a souvenir given to me early one morning shortly after moving to Casa. Five teenagers knocked at the kitchen door, the leader holding out the skull, which they were hoping to sell. "But where did you find it?" I inquired. "It came from the old ditch," they explained, meaning the irrigation ditch east of Casa, reputed to be the oldest in Corrales. I refused their offer. They wondered what to do, and I suggested they take it to the police. The idea frightened them so much that they pushed the skull in my hands and fled. Enrolled at the university at the time, I dropped it off in the Anthropology Department. Several months later I was informed that the skull was from a young man of twenty-plus years and was about two hundred years old.

The oratorio has celebrated weddings, held memorials, and received blessings. Monks from the Monastery of Christ in the Desert near Abiquiú, New Mexico, have visited it several times, once bringing supplies for a Mass.

< FIGURE 49
Greek Revival doors from Governor Connelly home, Peralta, 1870s. 86 3/8 × 76 × 6 1/4 in. (overall). Photograph by David Nufer. Gift of Ward Alan and Shirley Jolly Minge (1997.51.145).

MASTER BEDROOM

A few steps farther along the portal led to the master bedroom. Pete Smith made and installed doors, windows, and their frames, not only for this room but also for the weaving room across the plazuela, for the gatekeeper's room, and for the gran sala (see fig. 24). Double doors at either end of the portal came from private homes now gone or remodeled; those on the east enclosing that side of the gallery came from Governor Henry Connelly's home in Peralta, New Mexico, south of Albuquerque (fig. 49). Dr. Connelly, a wealthy merchant who served as territorial governor during Lincoln's presidency, built a large home, which has since been remodeled. Within the bedroom, a blue door leading into the bathroom came from the Loretto Convent in Santa Fe.

The intricate ceiling and bed molding were part of the San José purchase. I covered the walls with white gesso and mauve dado from clay found near Cuba, New Mexico. Simultaneously, I added a fireplace using traditional methods. Tony Garcia located an alacena with a family in Chical, near the Pueblo of Isleta (see Taylor and Bokides, *New*

Mexico Furniture, 1600–1940, page 66, plate 67). We kept small and miniature tinwork here along with several watercolor and crayon-colored saints, probably the work of children. Tony's uncle, Carlos Sena, constructed the wardrobe, which former owners had stripped of its original red paint (see Taylor and Bokides, *New Mexico Furniture, 1600–1940*, page 174, plate 168).

Once owned by Governor Manuel Armijo, the magnificent brass bed replaced the mundane double beds we had been using (fig. 50). Tony acquired this French creation from Cecilia Burton, a descendant of the Juan José Baca family in Socorro. I discovered later through contact with Armijo descendant John Colligan that an identical bed existed in Las Cruces, New Mexico. To solve the mystery created by two Armijo beds seemed impossible, but John located papers describing a trip made by Governor Armijo and a brother to New York after the Mexican-American War, and from there to Paris—where it was possible they purchased the beds, one for each. Governor W. W. H. Davis described a visit to Governor Armijo's residence in Lemitar, north of Socorro, shortly after the war: two beds were occupied by Armijo and guests after lunch and wines. Apparently the trip to Paris had not yet occurred, as no comments were left by Governor Davis about any such unusual bed.

Several extraordinary pieces of furniture occupied this room. One of my favorites was a plain, coarsely dovetailed box on its original stand, all pine. What was unusual were two rawhide bands wrapped neatly around the top and under the lid, meant obviously to reinforce the four planks. The chest came from Llano, New Mexico, east of Peñasco, all original and never painted (Taylor and Bokides, *New Mexico Furniture, 1600–1940*, page 47, plate 36). Similar wear and dovetailing existed on other boxes in the collection; see the large six-plank chest illustrated on page 47, plate 35 of Taylor and Bokides.

Another six-plank box, small and painted over with lacquer-like finish with florals and figures, was unusual for New Mexico. It had a simple lock, New Mexican made, and leather hinges. E. Boyd, in her *Popular Arts of Spanish New Mexico* (page 258), concluded that such boxes (there were only a few known) were made in New Mexico but

< FIGURE 50
French brass canopy bed owned by Governor Manuel Armijo, ca. 1845. 113 × 78 3/4 × 55 in. Photograph by David Nufer. Museum purchase, 1983 Government Obligation Bonds (1985.3.1).

> FIGURE 51
Hispanic New Mexican jerga from the Minge Collection, mid- to late nineteenth century. Photograph by Damian Andrus.

painted by a Mexican itinerant using oil paints. A second set of smaller boxes was entirely of leather, leather strips containing patches of red wool, and panels of green velvet, possibly silk. Because I had found a similar *petaca* described in a letter from Mexico in the seventeenth century, Francis Robinson (then curator of ancient and medieval art, Detroit Institute of Arts) was able to get some idea of its age. He presented Casa with one purchased from the Fred Harvey collections in Santa Fe.

Floor coverings in this room, the gran sala, weaving room, and library were known to the Spanish commonly as jerga, but the word had various spellings in colonial documents. Jerga was a homespun woolen material that weavers turned out in countless varas, and very few examples still exist (fig. 51). In Nora Fisher, ed., *Spanish Textile Tradition of New Mexico and Colorado*, Trish Spillman, in her essay "Jerga," states that the Minge Collection "surpasses that of any museum" (page 147). The essay gives extensive descriptions of this type of textile, its uses, designs, and much more. For a discussion of looms, see Fisher's essay "The Traditional Loom," with illustrations of Casa's treadle loom, circa 1775 (page 193, figure 1), and that loom's rare reeds (page 194, figure 2), which may be sole survivors from older looms.

GRAN SALA (BALLROOM)

The magnificent corbels supporting the vigas came from Tomé, New Mexico, and date to 1738–40 (see fig. 25). The Tomé church had been reroofed and had undergone other repairs in the 1890s, while the corbels were stored in a shed behind the church. Tony Garcia purchased surviving pieces in 1950, selling them to Eleanor Bedell, the owner of an antique shop in Santa Fe. Not having room at the shop, she had Tony take them to the backyard of her home, where they lay scattered about in the open, unprotected. After negotiating a price, Tony returned them to Albuquerque and our duplex on Princeton. The transaction took place during 1951 and 1952, constituting our first architectural acquisition.

Quite a number of the corbels were missing or spoiled by leaks, and Eleanor Bedell's shop had sold some. Remaining were two sizes and designs that measured, more or less, two and three varas long each. All had been finished by adz, and a few

butt-ends had colonial numbers scrolled in black. By this time, I realized I was being too "pure" in my approach to restoration, even though some corbels were missing. My attitude changed after a visit to the Cloisters in New York and my discovery of how many of the original building components had been replaced. Afterward, I was determined to replace the corbels and redo the roofing. Meanwhile, one could envision the stark beauty of the original ceiling.

The gran sala possessed several other unusual architectural elements. Sambullo (pintle) doors on the east wall, leading from the upstairs bedroom onto the balcony, were made at the Pueblo of Acoma. These appeared to be quite old and doubtless were crafted in a workshop at the mission.

Tony Garcia often mused that he found some of the oldest artifacts and architectural elements available in the Indian pueblos. An example of his claim was the window with its frame and shutters, which came from the Pueblo of Santa Ana, and which ended high on the south end of the room. Its wooden shutters had been mounted with pintle hinges. I assembled the balcony on the south wall, where my romantic inclinations envisioned children watching fiestas and bailes below. The stone paving was a gift from the Pueblo of Acoma. At the south door, friends from Acoma placed a marked stone with an arrow pointing toward the pueblo.

The sala also had some of the collection's older furnishings. We arranged chairs and low boxes around the room's walls, having been told by our neighboring Griegos and others that traditionally the arrangement allowed families to enjoy music and dancing. One of the boxes of six-plank construction had hides laced through its corners as reinforcements. The lacing ended in knots. On its front a rude incision survived; it was a representation of the Spanish dou-ble eagle. Judging from the large dovetailing and general wear, this chest saw two hundred years of use (See Taylor and Bokides, *New Mexico Furniture, 1600–1940*, page 47, plate 35).

Indian or Rio Grande blankets covered the low chests. Along the west wall stood one of the oldest chairs surviving in New Mexico, thought to have been used in the destroyed mission at the Pueblo of Taos (fig. 52). Taylor and Bokides dated the chair,

FIGURE 52
Hispanic New Mexican priest's chair collected in Taos Pueblo, ca. 1730. Photograph by David Nufer. Museum purchase, 1995 General Obligation Bonds (1998.20.22).

with its buffalo hide stretched along the back rail, to the early 1700s, likely made in a workshop in the Pueblo of Pecos (see Taylor and Bokides, *New Mexico Furniture, 1600–1940*, page 90, plate 102, and Francis J. Puig and Michael Conforti, eds., *The American Craftsman and the European Tradition, 1620–1820*, page 186, figure 3, and discussions).

On the north wall toward the northeast corner was a six-plank chest of unusual proportions. Unpainted and in excellent condition, with no checks or breaks, it was special for its planks measuring over thirty inches wide—minimalism superbly expressed. Above we placed an eighteenth-century bulto of Our Lady of Sorrows. Enclosed by a wooden niche or cage, painted in several colors, and topped with a beautifully carved wooden shell, she had hollow framing for the gown of canvas, and plaster and wood carved to make the upper body. A sword, possibly of silver, was missing from the breast. Tony Garcia purchased the shrine from a family in the Pueblo of Isleta.

Centered on the west wall sat another eighteenth-century framed chest with sophisticated ironwork. Simmons and Turley found the linked hasp "unusual" (see Simmons and Turley, *Southwestern Colonial Ironwork*, pages 146–47, plate 21). The native pine lid and bottom were one board each; the box, never painted, was in excellent condition. Taylor and Bokides described the ironwork as "extraordinary" (see page 58, plate 57).

I purchased the putti above the fireplace while a student in Mexico City. They were made by an indigenous person—a woodcarver, explained the dealer—and they

FIGURE 53
Gatekeeper's room with shepherd's bed, 2016. Photograph by Nora Vanesky.

decorated a village altar. He also pointed out they had been carved from cedar and covered with light plaster.

GATEKEEPER'S ROOM

Guard rooms were prevalent in parts of Mexico so they may have existed in early New Mexican forts, possibly at the Palace of Governors in Santa Fe. In any case, Casa received space ideally suited, located at the west entrance off the corral. Over the years I had set aside stray vigas, latillas, and a forked stanchion for framing a shepherd's bed over the fireplace. Beds arranged atop the structure received warmth from the fire below. I had a fireplace completed during the west wing construction, and subsequently built the framing supported on a platform of adobe and stone (fig. 53). We moved in the spring of 1997, before I could finish the project. For guidance, however, I had seen a shepherd's bed in the kitchen located off a plazuela in the "Casa en la Chaparral" (home out in the brush, so-called by residents in Bernalillo), west of the town and north of Corrales.

Linseed oil and turpentine produce a tough, leathery mud floor, durable and attractive, in contemporary adobe settings. This practice, or the much-debated use of blood mixed into the mud, were not traditional to my knowledge. Jesús Mendosa, on the other hand, was fully experienced in putting together a traditional mud floor. We gathered earth rich in clay and gunnysacks of chopped wheat straw, the latter purchased from the local feed store. So we proceeded, Jesús mixing mud and straw and delivering the mixture to the room where I was leveling and smoothing a mud slab some ten inches thick. We were finished in October, and I sealed the door with a pledge not to open the room until Christmas Eve.

During festivities that Christmas Eve, I told my extended family and friends that a surprise awaited. Eventually I was able to gather the group out in the zaguán. After describing the project of last October, and that the floor would by now be dry and hard, I opened the door and there by flashlight stood a rich green lawn of sprouting wheat! The door remained closed until late spring.

WEAVING ROOM

Immediately west of the library and opening onto the plazuela, the weaving room actually comprised two separate spaces. A substantial low wall divided the room, and in the larger of the two I planned to assemble both looms from the collections and to display textiles (fig. 54). The second space occupied about one-third of the east end—a work area created after installation of the trojas (grain storage bins), made of hand-adzed planks about two varas high and nearly six inches thick (fig. 55). Tony Garcia had found these rare bins in an abandoned adobe near Mora, New Mexico. I installed them in the arrangement they were in when he originally found them. A six-plank chest, which had been used for storing grain, rested over the east end. My plan was to move in metates and manos and other related tools used to prepare foodstuffs for the main kitchen.

< FIGURE 54
Hispanic New Mexican frazada / El Valle blanket, 1890–1910. 82 × 47 × 1/4 in. Photograph by David Nufer. Museum purchase, 1995 Government Obligation Bonds (1998.19.41).

FIGURE 55
Weaving room, east end, 2012. Photograph by David Nufer.

Toward the west end, I came to use the largest space as my office. I had a fireplace and wood-burning stove near my desk. The looms were not moved into place while we occupied Casa, because in addition to the desk we had other family pieces there, including a piano, a harp, and the pump organ that had belonged to my great-grandfather, who had homesteaded in Kansas just after the Civil War (fig. 56).

According to documents in the New Mexico Records and Archives Center, the Spanish government had conducted a census of looms, many of them found in family homes. The oldest of the two Tony Garcia found for me came from near Española, New Mexico, near Hernández, where the owner claimed it to be eighteenth century. The purchase included a box with assorted tools and spare parts, along with its original reeds. For further discussion of New Mexican looms, including this one, see Nora Fisher, ed., *Spanish Textile Tradition of New Mexico and Colorado*, pages 192–95, figures 1 and 2.

FIGURE 56
Weaving room, west end, 2012.
Photograph by David Nufer.

Tony located a second loom in Lemitar, just north of Socorro. He purchased it from Luz Chávez, with samples of weaving made by ancestors on the same loom. Luz believed it to have been made by a great-great-grandfather around 1825, and among samples sold was a scarce Rio Abajo cotton blanket (figs. 57 and 58). For illustrations and discussion of this loom and blanket, see Deborah C. Slaney, *Wonders of the Weavers: Nineteenth-Century Río Grande Weavings from the Collection of the Albuquerque Museum*, pages 46–47, plate 15, and pages 96–99.

BIBLIOTECA (LIBRARY)

Books on the Southwest made up a large portion of the library collection. Discussions with museum officials, during negotiations for transferring Casa to the City of Albuquerque, clarified our wish for the library to be used as a research center for people interested in Spanish Colonial life in New Mexico. Accumulated here were a number of scarce items and curious objects related to the state's history.

The Pueblo pottery collection eventually grew to represent work from most of the pueblos and included examples from prehistory to the present day (figs. 59, 60, and 61). A counter from an old store in San Miguel, New Mexico, stood facing the east wall. It held "life and death" boxes containing family papers; tobacco canteens of leather, brass, and silver; an early daguerreotype

FIGURE 57

Chávez family, Hispanic New Mexican Rio Abajo cotton blanket from Lemitar, ca. 1825. 81 × 50 × 1/4 in. Photograph by David Nufer. Museum purchase, 1995 General Obligation Bonds (1998.20.9).

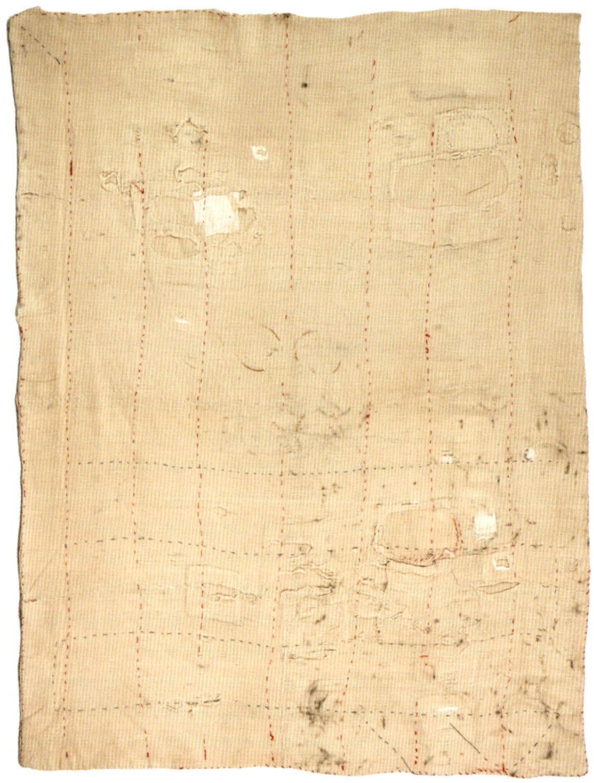

FIGURE 58

Chávez family, Hispanic New Mexican wool colchón *from Lemitar, 1800–1830. 75 3/4 × 57 1/2 × 1 in. Photograph by David Nufer. Museum purchase, 1995 General Obligation Bonds (1998.19.47).*

FIGURE 59

Ancestral Pueblo jar, Agua Fria Glaze-on-red, 1350–1450. 11 × 14 1/2 in. Photograph by David Nufer. Museum purchase, 1995 General Obligation Bonds (1998.22.17)

FIGURE 60

Acoma polychrome jar, ca. 1870. 12 13/16 × 13 3/16 in. Photograph by David Nufer. Museum purchase, 1995 General Obligation Bonds (1998.21.44).

FIGURE 61

Zia polychrome dough bowl, ca. 1880. 11 5/16 × 18 1/4 in. Photograph by David Nufer. Museum purchase, 1995 General Obligation Bonds (1998.23.13).

FIGURE 62
Daguerreotype from the family of Father Antonio José Martínez, Taos. 4 1/8 × 3 1/4 × 1 in. (closed). Photograph by Heugh-Edmondson Conservation. Museum purchase, 1995 General Obligation Bonds (1998.27.29).

of Father Antonio José Martínez (fig. 62); and a back plate—part of Spanish armor that Will Prince, son of Governor Bradford Prince, claimed came from the Camino Real (Royal Road) somewhere between Socorro and El Paso, and had been given to the governor by Adolph Bandelier. The case also held a statue of Daedalus, the first successful man of flight, a gift from Pete's wife, Patricia Smith; a feather box from a pueblo; a small hollowed log and lid; a pair of cockfighting spurs in their original cases; and the horno model made for us by Rose and Joe Ray and their grandchildren. Obviously, the *biblioteca* became a place for curios (figs. 63–65).

In the northwest corner stood an eight-foot barber pole with coats of red and white; it came from Española. Next to the pole and fireplace was a unique safe made for Governor Manuel Armijo (fig. 66). Tony purchased it from Cecilia Burton in Socorro, who had inherited it with a number of Governor Armijo's personal belongings (figs. 67a and 67b). She told Tony that the family had lent the safe to the US Army during the Civil War, and that it had been used at Fort Craig south of Socorro. Heavy wooden doors opened to reveal eight sizable drawers, marked to hold different species of coins: francs, half-dollars, and gold pieces. The entire safe was encrusted with wrought nails and great ironwork, and a lacquer-like black paint covered the entire box. Because one of the drawers had been designated for francs, it has been thought by some to have been made during the early Santa Fe Trail days.

FIGURE 63
Hispanic New Mexican document box by José María Apodaca (left) with document or trinket boxes, 1880–1900. 9 15/16 × 8 9/16 × 5 7/8 in.; 8 5/16 × 5 1/2 × 5 in. Photograph by Damian Andrus. Museum purchase, 1995 Government Obligation Bonds. Gift of Ward Alan and Shirley Jolly Minge (left, 1998.18.7; right, 1997.51.120).

FIGURE 64
Hispanic New Mexican or Mexican rocker-engraved silver bracelets, one engraved "Antonia Chabes," mid- to late nineteenth century. 1 × 3 1/2 × 2 1/2 in. (average). Photograph by Damian Andrus. Museum purchase, 1995 General Obligation Bonds (left to right: 1998.28.2, 3, 5, 6, and 4).

FIGURE 65
Hispanic New Mexican gold filigree necklace from Abeitia Jewelers, Socorro, mid- to late nineteenth century. 15 × 1 3/4 × 1/2 in. (unclasped). Photograph by David Nufer. Museum purchase, 1995 General Obligation Bonds (1998.27.44).

FIGURE 66
Alfred S. Waugh, French. Pastel portrait of Governor Manuel Armijo, ca. 1846. 23 × 19 in. (sight). Photograph by David Nufer. Museum purchase, 1995 Government Obligation Bonds (1998.22.51).

a

b

FIGURES 67 a AND 67 b
Safe owned by Governor Manuel Armijo, 1841–45. Photographs by David Nufer. 41 × 45 × 21 3/4 in. (closed). Museum purchase, 1995 General Obligation Bonds (1998.22.35.a).

Aside from bookcases, other furnishings included a somewhat older table set against the west wall between the fireplace and the southwest corner. It came from an abandoned church west of Anton Chico, New Mexico (see Taylor and Bokides, *New Mexico Furniture, 1600–1940*, page 72, plate 78). Between bookcases along the south wall was one of the finest surviving harineros (there were a number of them in the collections, with four being quite large). Harineros functioned as grain cribs or bins. This special harinero, found in the Ranchitos area near Belén, New Mexico, is made of pine with slab metal hinges and dates to 1800, possibly earlier. I had rubbed the top and sides by hand, hard enough to create heat and absorb body oil for a lasting rich finish.

No colonial item was more attractive than my favorite alacena on the north wall. Tony Garcia discovered it in an eighteenth-century "crumbling" adobe at Rancho de Taos, and he showed up with the piece as the library was in progress. No nails had been used, or dowels, but by including metal hinges as a small latch, the carpenter had produced a special piece. Walls were high enough so that I could hollow out a space for the cupboard toward the northwest corner. Once the assembled parts were

> FIGURE 68
Hispanic New Mexican three-piece jerga, ca. 1850–90. 144 × 60 × 1/4 in. Photograph by David Nufer. Gift of Ward Alan and Shirley Jolly Minge (1998.25.23).

wrapped tightly with twine, the alacena slipped into the space and was shimmed and mudded around the openings. The carpenter had sculpted the parts with adz and drawknife and had painted the surface with a water-soluble dark brown.

A large Federal-style entry was a gift from architect George Pearl. He had been contracted to work on the Luna family home on the east side of Los Lunas, where it had been moved from the center of town when the railroad passed through in the 1880s. George learned from the owners that woodwork, including the doorway, had been moved from a much older adobe on the plaza at a time when the family wanted to build some distance from the railroad. Architects visiting Casa since its installation speculate that the original owners had been influenced by homes they had seen during trips to Saint Louis, Kansas City, or Saint Joseph, Missouri—departing points for Santa Fe Trail traders as early as 1820s.

Pete Smith and crew installed the doorway and replaced the double doors. They installed shutters, which were made by Albuquerque santero Frank Ortiz, on the gran sala windows. On the shutters' walls were placed matching sets of New Mexican colonial shutter dogs, the only ones I've seen that were forged locally.

Carmen Espinosa, a doyenne of the Spanish Colonial arts highly regarded in Albuquerque circles, requested a tour—at the same time refusing lunch or refreshments. As we passed from room to room I sensed her pleasure in all the familiar things from her own life. "But Alan," she finally remarked, "you have no traditional black-and-white banded jergas." I did not respond, but when at last we entered the library she took my arm in tears because, spread before us, was the carpeting she had hoped to find here (fig. 68). A week or so later her letter arrived, written in Spanish, telling me how the experience had reminded her of an uncle's old adobe where she had spent many happy days as a girl.

GLOSSARY

acequia: Irrigation ditch

adobe: Sun-dried mud and straw brick used as a building material

alacena: Cupboard, set into the wall

Ancestral Pueblo: Native American culture that emerged throughout the Four Corners region of the Southwest

arado: Plow

armario: Armoire used for storage, clothing storage

asador: Iron spit for roasting meat

baile: Dance, with musicians

banco: Bench; furniture sometimes built into a wall

biblioteca: Library

bulto: Three-dimensionally carved saint

buttress: Adobe wall support

caja: Box or chest used for storage

camposanto: Cemetery; burial plot in front of a church

carpintero: Carpenter, woodworker

casa: House; home

cazo: Cauldron or pot; also, ladle

ceja: Ridge line; cliff

chabacano: Apricot tree

chamisa: Shrub used as a dye and a stuffing for ceilings and jerga

cocina: Kitchen

colchón: Mattress cover

comal: Large, flat stone griddle for making piki bread, tortillas, and other types of food

comedor: Dining room

corbel: Carved wooden support used between posts and vigas to support the ceiling and roof of a room or portal

Corrales: Corrals, enclosed areas for animals and equipment; the village in which Casa San Ysidro is located

dado: A long wooden horizontal beam between the wall and roof that spreads the load of the roof

dispensa: Storeroom for supplies and equipment; toolshed

doyenne: A woman who is most respected or prominent in her field

escusado: Outhouse; toilet

fiesta: Party or celebration

fogón: Indoor fireplace or hearth

< Casa San Ysidro, 2016. Photograph by Gene Peach.

frazada: Blanket or lap robe

galería: Central passageway or breezeway

garambullos: Black currants and other small berries

gesso; also yeso: A mixture of gypsum and animal glue applied to the wood of retablos or bultos prior to painting

Greek Revival: A Territorial period architectural style featuring a central breezeway and triangular pediments, sometimes in adobe or terrón construction in the Southwest

hacienda: A large compound of multiple dwellings used as artisans' workshops

harinero: Grain chest

horno: Outdoor adobe oven

jerga; gerga: Wool sack cloth, fabric, or carpeting woven on a horizontal loom

latillas: Small branches used in fences and ceilings

mano: Ancestral Pueblo or Mexican hand stone used for grinding corn in metates

Manzano: Apple; village near where Casa's front door and barn were found

membrillo: Quince tree

metate: Ancestral Pueblo or Mexican stone slab or trough for grinding corn

morada: Local chapel or meeting house for Los Hermanos, the Penitente Brotherhood

nicho: Shelf or cabinet, sometimes built into a wall

oratorio: Chapel

peón; peones: Laborer; farmhand

petaca: Mexican hide, wood, and fabric trunk used for storage

pintle: Carved wooden pin extending from the bottom and top edges of a window or door, extending into adobe, wood, or stone, allowing it to swivel without metal hinges

Placitas: Little plazas; also the village in which several of Casa's earthen pigments are found

plazuela: Local Spanish for central patio inside a building

portal: Covered porch that creates shade

portón: Door or gate; an opening (see puertón)

pretiles: parapets; firewalls

puerta: Door or gate; an opening

puertón: Local term for gate that allows entry through the zaguán (see portón)

putti: Cherubs

rancho: Ranch house or farmhouse

reredos: Altarpiece, screen, or decoration behind the altar in a church

retablo: A painting on wood, metal, or fabric, usually of a saint

sala: Also gran sala; ballroom, parlor, or receiving area for guests

sala para la familia: Family room; parlor

sambullo: Window with pintle hinges

San Ysidro Labrador: Saint Isidore the Farmer, patron saint of Corrales, New Mexico

santero: An artisan who makes bultos and retablos of Catholic saints

Siete Hermanas, las: The Seven Sisters; heritage climbing roses

tabla: Flat roofing plank, laid over vigas

tarima: Stool made of adzed planks on legs

Territorial period: The period when New Mexico was a territory of the United States, from 1850 to 1912

terrón; terrones: Brick of sod cut from river terraces for use in building construction

trastero: An upright cabinet used for storage

troja: Interior storage bin

vara: Unit of Spanish measurement, approximately thirty-three inches

viga: Log used as a roofing beam

zaguán: Entrance to a compound leading to a plazuela or corral

Zócalo: Main square in central Mexico City

BIBLIOGRAPHY

Armstrong, Ruth. "The Most Victorian Christmas Tree in New Mexico." *New Mexico Magazine* (December 1980), 30.

Boston Museum of Fine Arts. *Frontier America: The Far West*. Boston: Museum of Fine Arts, 1975.

Boyd, E. *Popular Arts of Spanish New Mexico*. Santa Fe: Museum of New Mexico Press, 1974.

Cobos, Rubén. *A Dictionary of New Mexico and Southern Colorado Spanish*. Santa Fe: Museum of New Mexico Press, 1983.

Cohen, Elizabeth. "Saving Grace, Preserving and Restoring Historic Homes." *Albuquerque Monthly*. Homes issue (June 1996). Photography by Hickey-Robertson.

Conron, John. "A Hacienda Recreated, Beauty and Comfort Out of the Past." *New Mexico Magazine* (winter 1991). Photography by John Candelaria.

Coulter, Lane, and Maurice M. Dixon Jr., *New Mexican Tinwork, 1840–1940*. Albuquerque: University of New Mexico Press, 1990.

Davis, Mary P., and the Corrales Historical Society. *Images of America: Corrales*. Charleston, SC: Arcadia Publishing, 2010.

DellaFlora, Anthony. "House of History." *Albuquerque Journal*, April 30, 1995.

Dixon, Maurice M., Jr., *The Artistic Odyssey of Higinio Gonzales: A Tinsmith and Poet in Territorial New Mexico*. Norman: University of Oklahoma Press, 2015.

Fairbanks, Jonathan L., and Elizabeth Bidwell Bates. *American Furniture 1620 to the Present*, 428–31, 434. New York: Richard Marek Publishers, 1981.

Fisher, Nora, comp. and ed. *Spanish Textile Tradition of New Mexico and Colorado*. Santa Fe: Museum of New Mexico Press, 1994.

Garcia, Tony. *The Beginning of the Casa San Ysidro in Corrales, New Mexico, and the Provenance of Its Spanish Colonial Artifacts*. Albuquerque: self-published, n.d.

< *Dining room, 2011. Photograph by David Nufer.*

Gillette, W. Dean. "Casa San Ysidro: Restored Spanish Colonial Hacienda in New Mexico." *Southern Accents* 11, no. 5 (November–December 1988).

Grassham, John W. "Casa San Ysidro: The Gutiérrez/Minge House." In "American Furniture and Decorative Arts from Spain's Northern Frontier, 1700–1900, Catalogue of Mr. and Mrs. Al Luckett, Jr., New York." *Sotheby's*, January 15, 1998.

Hammett, Kingsley H. *Early New Mexican Furniture: A Handbook of Plans and Building Techniques*. Santa Fe: Fleetwood Press, 1999.

Larese, Steve. "Corrales' Casa San Ysidro." *New Mexico Magazine*. Special homes issue (May 1999).

Mather, Christine. "Casa San Ysidro: Preservation and Reconstruction of an 18th Century New Mexico Hacienda; An Introduction to Casa San Ysidro." Albuquerque: Albuquerque Museum, n.d.

———. "Living with Antiques: Casa San Ysidro, Corrales, New Mexico." *Antiques* (April 1978), 820–29.

Minge, Ward Alan, and Simon Ortiz. *Acoma, Pueblo in the Sky*. Albuquerque: University of New Mexico Press, 1991.

Neary, John. "Casa San Ysidro." *Americana* (November 1975), 2–7.

Nestor, Sarah. *Spanish Textile Tradition of New Mexico and Colorado*. Santa Fe: Museum of New Mexico Press, 1979.

Pierce, Donna L. "New Mexico Furniture and Its Spanish Prototypes." In *The American Craftsman and the European Tradition, 1620–1820*, edited by Francis J. Puig and Michael Conforti. Minneapolis: Minneapolis Institute of Arts; Hanover, NH: distributed by the University Press of New England, 1989.

Puig, Francis J., and Michael Conforti, eds. *The American Craftsman and the European Tradition, 1620–1820*. Minneapolis: Minneapolis Institute of Arts; Hanover, NH: distributed by the University Press of New England, 1989.

Rawlings, Irene M.K. "Casa San Ysidro." *Better Homes and Gardens Country Home* (April 1986), 89–98.

Shearer, Mike. "Casa San Ysidro, an 18th-Century Hacienda." *New Mexico Magazine* (November 1984). Photography by Robert Reck.

Simmons, Marc, and Frank Turley. *Southwestern Colonial Ironwork: The Spanish Blacksmithing Tradition from Texas to California*. Santa Fe: Museum of New Mexico Press, 1980.

Slaney, Deborah C. *Wonders of the Weavers/Maravillas de los tejedores: Nineteenth-Century Río Grande Weavings from the Collection of the Albuquerque Museum*. Albuquerque: Albuquerque Museum, 2005.

Taylor, Lonn, and Dessa Bokides. *New Mexico Furniture, 1600–1940*. Santa Fe: Museum of New Mexico Press, 1987.

Wilson, Chris. "Casa San Ysidro (Gutiérrez/Minge House) Docent Workshop." Unpublished typescript, September 1998.

———. "Draft National Register Nomination for the Gutiérrez-Minge House (Casa San Ysidro)." Unpublished typescript, May 23, 1997.

INDEX

Page numbers in *italics* refer to illustrations.

< José Rafael Aragón, Hispanic New Mexican retablo, San Ysidro Labrador, 1820–60.